NAVAL HISTORY IN THE LAW COURTS

A Selection of Old Maritime Cases

BY

WILLIAM SENIOR

Of the Middle Temple, Barrister-at-Law

THE LAWBOOK EXCHANGE, LTD.
Clark, New Jersey

ISBN 9781584779414

Lawbook Exchange edition 2011

The quality of this reprint is equivalent to the quality of the original work.

THE LAWBOOK EXCHANGE, LTD.
33 Terminal Avenue
Clark, New Jersey 07066-1321

*Please see our website for a selection of our other publications
and fine facsimile reprints of classic works of legal history:*
www.lawbookexchange.com

Library of Congress Cataloging-in-Publication Data

Senior, William, 1861-1930.
  Naval history in the law courts : a selection of old maritime cases
/ by William Senior.
      p. cm.
  Includes bibliographical references and index.
  Originally published: London, New York : Longmans, Green,
1927.
  ISBN-13: 978-1-58477-941-4 (cloth : alk. paper)
  ISBN-10: 1-58477-941-1 (cloth : alk. paper)
  1. Trials--Great Britain. 2. Great Britain--History, Naval. I. Title.
  KD1815.S46 2009
  343.4209'6--dc22
                                    2008044523

Printed in the United States of America on acid-free paper

NAVAL HISTORY IN THE LAW COURTS

A Selection of Old Maritime Cases

BY

WILLIAM SENIOR
Of the Middle Temple, Barrister-at-Law

LONGMANS, GREEN AND CO. LTD.
39 PATERNOSTER ROW, LONDON, E.C. 4
NEW YORK, TORONTO
CALCUTTA, BOMBAY AND MADRAS
1927

PREFACE

IN his *History of the Criminal Law* the late
Mr. Justice Stephen said of certain old trials
that they set the manners of the time before
the reader with an authenticity and life in his
opinion more curious and entertaining than any
romance ever written. These narratives of litiga-
tion arising out of things done upon the sea
in days gone by must needs lack the flavour of
contemporary records such as evoked the Judge's
admiring comparison. Yet as they have been
fashioned for the most part out of similar documents my hope is that the manners of those who
have used the sea at the various times they cover,
though here set before the reader at second-hand,
may still be found both ' curious and entertaining.'

W. S.

THE seventh and two last chapters in this book have appeared in *The Cornhill Magazine*, and my thanks are due to the Editor for permission to use them.

CONTENTS

I

DRAKE AT THE SUIT OF DOUGHTY

CHRONOLOGICAL order compels me to begin this collection of trials with a story of some legal proceedings which never came to a trial. The circumstance that they were nipped in the bud by Queen Elizabeth herself, in the interest of so outstanding a hero in English history as Sir Francis Drake, may perhaps excuse an interrogative ending.

It will be remembered that early in the course of Drake's famous voyage of circumnavigation in the *Golden Hind,* one Thomas Doughty, a volunteer with the squadron, was placed under arrest, and upon the arrival of the expedition at Port St. Julian on the south-east coast of South America, was tried upon charges of insubordination, found guilty and executed. The propriety of Drake's action has been much canvassed. His defenders usually suggest that he held a commission from the Crown empowering him to administer military law. The legal proceedings which were taken against Drake almost immediately after his return by Doughty's brother John, who had also accompanied the expedition, are material to that supposition, inasmuch as the production of such a commission would, *prima facie,* have been a good answer to them. Had Drake been provided with a commission in terms similar to those in the letters-patent which were drafted for the projected voyage of Grenville and his companions in 1574, expressly giving them power of life and death over " persons of the companye rebellyously or obstinatly resisting against there commandements or aucthorytie," that fact alone, whether it did or did not render the conviction and punishment of Thomas Doughty a *chose jugée*, would at least have made the argument that it had done so the first to be advanced against anyone attempting to reopen the matter. One would therefore expect to find in what is recorded of John Doughty's law-suit by men who remembered it some mention of the point. But so far as appears it was not taken. The only inference to be drawn is that there was nothing upon which to found it.

With Drake's treatment of Thomas Doughty we are concerned chiefly as leading to John Doughty's action. Froude, of course, whilst admitting there is no proof of it, insinuates that Thomas was a secret agent of Philip of Spain or the Jesuits. No one knows. Our business is first with the curious legal aftermath of a celebrated voyage.

John Doughty's futile effort to have the law of Drake has been very little noticed, probably because nobody imagined that the laconic law-reports of the seventeenth century could anywise eke out the material of the naval historian. It is true that the late Sir Julian Corbett has cited the allusion to Doughty's case which was made by Sir Edward Coke during a debate on martial law in the House of Commons in 1628, and which

is epitomised by Rushworth as follows : " Drake
slew Doughty beyond sea. Doughty's brother
desired an appeal (of murder) in the Constable
and Marshal's Court. Resolved by Wray (Sir
Christopher Wray, then Lord Chief Justice) and
the other judges he may sue there." " By this
curious chance," adds Sir Julian, " we know that
the assertion which has always been made, that
the execution of Doughty was never called in
question, is not true." But having thus referred
to the fact that the full court of the Queen's
Bench held that John Doughty was entitled to
proceed with his " appeal " in the Court of
Chivalry, as the tribunal of the Constable and
Marshal was called, the author of *Drake and
the Tudor Navy* did not pursue the matter
further. It is possible, however, to explain why
John Doughty failed, in spite of this decision of
the Queen's Bench that *prima facie* he had a
right to try his fortune in the courts. It was not
upon the production of Drake's commission, for
no such document was ever mentioned. Nor
was it upon the merits of the case, for he never
got a hearing. He was non-suited upon a
technical point of law which Elizabeth by a few
strokes of her pen could have rendered non-
existent had she pleased.

Two lawyers, Sir Edward Coke and Sir Richard
Hutton, both of whom were living in 1581 when
Doughty instituted his proceedings, and both
of whom afterwards became judges, have left a
brief note of them. Coke had already been called
to the Bar in 1578. Hutton was called in 1586,
but would have been old enough four or five

years earlier to be interested in the case as a student. Neither of them at any rate had any other kind of interest in it. Each of them records it as illustrating legal procedure in a book intended purely for the guidance of their profession. Had Drake's commission been pleaded in bar of a suit that these learned authors deemed interesting enough thus to record, it is strange that they should not have mentioned the fact.

In order that the reader unacquainted with legal history may appreciate precisely what happened, it is desirable first of all that some explanation should be given of the nature of the action that Doughty wished to take, and of the now long-obsolete court which he tried to set in motion. . An " appeal of felony " or of " murder " in the old law had nothing to do with an appeal from one court to another and a higher one—the sense in which we in modern times commonly use the word : from an early date the verb *appellare* was used to describe the action of one who brings a criminal charge against another. And in such an appeal the accuser had as a general rule to offer battle. Trial by battle was a method of trial by no means peculiar to the special tribunal to which Doughty, for reasons that will be presently apparent, had recourse. It might be had at common law, and it was not expressly abolished there until the year 1819, though by that time it had long fallen into desuetude. " Judicial combat in criminal cases is allowed," says Selden, " for the trial of a particular objected misdeed, cognizable by the ordinary course of common law . . . it is likewise permitted for the purgation of an offence against military honour, which the high court of chivalry is to marshal by the law of arms." But if the " objected misdeed " related to military matters and also had taken place outside the realm the only proper tribunal to try it was the Court of the Constable and Marshal. Even Coke, who constantly displays in his writings a marked dislike to every jurisdiction lying outside the domain of the English common law, admits this. " If a subject of the King be killed by another of his subjects out of England in any foreine country," he says, " the wife or he that is heire of the dead may have an appeale for this murder or homicide before the Constable and Marshal." This is in accordance with what the Queen's Bench judges had ruled in the particular case with which we are concerned. It may be assumed that John Doughty was prepared to prove the requisite relationship to the deceased, and it will probably be now clear that in the circumstances of Thomas Doughty's death, the only road open to the would-be prosecutor lay through the Court of the Constable and Marshal. It is also to be noted that John Doughty was not bringing an appeal in our sense from a judgment of Drake in a court-martial constituted under a commission, but initiating a criminal charge as between subject and subject. The form of his proceedings is not without significance.

Now let us see how he would have to begin. The mode of trial began by a cartel or challenge containing the accusation, which was " exhibited " or presented to the judge of the Marshal's Court

B

and concluded with a statement by the appellant that he was ready to maintain the same by his body. The appellant was also required to swear to the truth of the cartel and that he was not actuated by malice : and if, after due consideration of the circumstances alleged, the combat was granted, notice was sent by the officers of the court to the accused person. We need not go into the various methods by which the appearance of the latter was obtained, or into what happened if he contumaciously ignored the notice. I do not know whether Sir Francis Drake was served with the process of the Earl Marshal's Court ; but if he was it would probably be difficult for a newly made knight altogether to disregard the summons of a court of Chivalry and Honour. Sir Julian Corbett, in his allusion to John Doughty's proceedings, assumes that it was Drake who took action before the Court of Queen's Bench in the hope of having them quashed. This seems probable : the only other explanation of the case coming before the Lord Chief Justice would be that Doughty, desirous to proceed in the Marshal's Court, himself moved the Queen's Bench for leave to sue there. It is of little consequence which happened : although in a subsequent case to which reference will presently be made, the common-law Judges were in like manner consulted beforehand. The important point to notice is that Doughty got his leave.

We have next to consider the character of the Court of the Constable and Marshal. It ought to be said that this tribunal, though an existing

institution even in the sixteenth century, was
not very often resorted to : and we cannot do
better than transcribe the description of it given
by Sir William Blackstone in his Commentaries.
" The Court of Chivalry," he says, " which was
a military court cr court of honour when held
before the Earl Marshal only, was also a
criminal court when held before the Lord High
Constable of England jointly with the Earl
Marshal. And then it had jurisdiction over
pleas of life and member arising in matters
of arms and deeds of war as well out of
the realm as within it." This difference of
jurisdiction between the Marshal sitting alone
and the court composed of both Constable and
Marshal was the rock upon which Doughty's
case split. Blackstone proceeds (he is writing in
1765) " but the criminal as well as the civil
part of its authority is fallen into entire disuse :
there having been no permanent High Constable
of England (but only *pro hac vice* at coronations
and the like) since the attainder and execution
of Stafford, Duke of Buckingham, 13 Hen. 8."
There was no one holding the office of High
Constable of England in 1581. The Earl Marshal
by himself might deprive you of coat-armour
for unknightly conduct, but he was not, unless
the Lord High Constable sat with him, a criminal
court.

An old statute of the year 1399 (1. Hen. IV.
cap. 14) had ordained in terms " that all appeals
to be made of things done out of the realm shall
be tried and determined before the Constable
and Marshal of England for the time being."

For the trial of such cases the court must be constituted by the joinder of both officers. This was recognised as the law in a similar case (except that it was an appeal of high treason committed in Germany) which occurred in the reign of Charles the First, and may be read in the State Trials. At that time, as a preliminary step, the Judges were consulted, and they resolved that the trial might be by an appeal of Treason, on which the Combat might be joined : but the King, they said, must make a Constable, *durante bene placito*, for the Marshal could not take the appeal without him. Accordingly in this case Charles appointed the Earl of Lindsey Lord High Constable *pro tempore*. It is immaterial to our present purpose that these much later proceedings were not carried through. A Lord High Constable was in fact created. In the appeal of John Doughty against Sir Francis Drake Elizabeth declined to supply the necessary reinforcement to the only tribunal that, so constituted, would have had jurisdiction. " It was resolved " says Sir Edward Coke, in his *Commentaries*, " in the raigne of Queen Elizabeth, in the case of Sir Francis Drake, who strook off the head of Dowtie *in partibus transmarinis*, that his brother and heire might have an appeale. *Sed regina noluit constituere constabularium Angliæ &c. et ideo dormivit appellum.*" We learn from the *Reports* of Sir Richard Hutton the further fact that " Petition was made to the Queen *by the Heir* to make a Constable but she would not."

There is nothing surprising in this ; it must have been a pretty hopeless petition from the start. Elizabeth's instructions to Mr. Tremayne to allow Drake to extract his ten thousand pounds from the treasure in the hold of the *Golden Hind* before the inventory was made had already been given at the end of 1580 ; and in April, 1581, she had knighted the person now accused. Nor can it be overlooked that the accuser, Master John Doughty, had been in some sort of trouble in 1576, before the expedition started ; there is on record his appeal to Leicester in the autumn of that year praying him to intercede with the Council for his release from the common gaol, " a very noysom place, replenished with misery." But what does seem curious is that John was only suppressed after all this legal pother, if in fact the Queen had already authorised Drake to pass judgment on Thomas.

We hear little of John Doughty after his failure to bring Drake before a court of justice, but that little is characteristic of the times. In May, 1582, Drake laid an information against him for words uttered on the occasion of the former's receipt of knighthood : and simultaneously comes evidence, obtained from one Patrick Mason, under torture, of a Spanish plot against Drake in which John Doughty was alleged to be implicated. He must have been thrown into prison very shortly afterwards, because when in October of the following year he petitioned the Council from the Marshalsea that he might be either " charged and called to answer " or set at liberty, he said he had then lain there for sixteen months. That petition was endorsed " Not to be released," and the rest is silence.

The purpose of this chapter is, however, complete with the tracing of John Doughty's proceedings against Drake a little further than, as far as I know, they have hitherto been followed, and in pointing out that nowhere in the course of them does any reference appear to have been made to the investment of Drake with power of life and death over Thomas Doughty or any other mutineer amongst his company. For the reason already mentioned it is difficult to account for that omission in the writings of lawyers, had such a power been expressly granted to the " General " by letters-patent before he sailed. We have, of course, always been entitled to draw the same inference from the general absence of any contemporary English reference to Drake's commission, which, had it ever existed, might have been set up in excuse for an act that, according to Camden, was being publicly blamed at the time ; but that it was not set up in answer to specific proceedings at law seems to render the inference still stronger.

I am far from saying that where so much is mysterious these considerations are conclusive : but in any unbiassed examination of the Doughty affair they would probably have weight. At the same time it is well to point out that they are merely concerned with the legal backing Drake may or may not have had *in re* Thomas Doughty, and not with his justice. The question of commission or no commission has not all the importance sometimes ascribed to it from the latter point of view, especially by writers bent above everything else upon making out a case on behalf

of a national hero. Supposing it to be established
that Drake held a commission to administer
martial law, it would not follow that Thomas
Doughty had a fair trial. There is said to have
been a jury impannelled to try him, a fact inconsistent with a court-martial : the members
of it were necessarily drawn from amongst
Drake's company, a circumstance which would
hardly make for their independence. Juries at
this period, even at home and in the ordinary
course of the criminal law, were, especially in
cases of treason, expected to do as they were
told. The jury that acquitted Sir N. Throck-
morton of treason in 1554 was severely fined :
thus assuring the conviction of Sir J. Throck-
morton upon the same evidence on which his
brother had been acquitted. On the other hand,
some measure of disciplinary authority over his
people, and that of a lawful kind, Drake must
necessarily have had. Even in these democratic
days there has to be conceded to every uncommissioned master-mariner upon the high seas a
modicum of such authority : it is inherent in his
office, and is, moreover, derived from that of
the State whose flag he flies. There is no other
source from which, in course of law, it can, or
ever could be, derived. The sixteenth century
was not democratic or overmuch concerned about
the liberty of the subject, nor was the distinction
between a public and a private ship as well
defined as it is now. That Sir Francis Drake was
high-handed and prone to exaggerate the powers
he rightly had we know from what happened
afterwards in the case of Vice-Admiral Borough,

wherein again the Doughty affair was remembered as an exercise of authority without warrant. In the phrase of a German historian the Tudor period was one of "enlightened absolutism." It is little wonder if Sir Francis Drake had assimilated something of the atmosphere in which he lived, and of which this very story is an illustration.

II

SALLEE ROVERS AT WINCHESTER

ON the 31st October, 1636, there was a remarkable trial-at-law at Winchester which throws
light at once upon the legal and maritime peculiari-
ties of the time. It was held before an unusual
tribunal, the court of the Vice-Admiral for the
coasts of Hampshire and the Isle of Wight, and
the prisoners who stood together in the dock
charged with murder and piracy were an unusual
agglomeration, made up of eleven Moors from
Sallee, four renegade Flemings or Dutchmen who
had "turned Turk," and a single Englishman,
one John Dunton of London, mariner.

The events that led up to this trial form only
one of many stories that might be told illustrating
the insecurity of the Narrow Seas about the
beginning of the reign of Charles the First : but
we are here concerned first of all only with the fate
of a small merchantman of London, called the
Little David, which had sailed out of the Thames
bound for the colony of Virginia. She had on
board seven women and fifty men and boys,
amongst them the John Dunton just mentioned,
and his little son nine years old. Their westerly
voyage was short : the *Little David* was but
thirty-five leagues past Land's End when she
was captured by a Moorish pirate and taken into
Sallee, where the whole of her passengers and

crew was sold into slavery. It was no uncommon occurrence : such depredations by the " Turks," as they were called, had then been going on for at least ten years. During all that time the authorities of the maritime towns in the West of England had been periodically begging for naval protection for their trade. There were the ship-money fleets, of course, but they were singularly ineffective in putting a stop to the trouble, and their maintenance led, as everybody knows, to troubles of another sort with which this story has nothing to do. Only a year before the date of the trial of this strange company of wrong-doers at Winchester, the Mayor of Plymouth had written to the Privy Council reporting the presence of a large squadron of Moslem marauders off Scilly, lying in wait for the fishing fleet returning from Newfoundland. In the very autumn of the year in which our story really begins the Mayors of Exeter, Plymouth, Barnstaple and other towns had told the Council that the pirates of Sallee were now so " numerous, strong and nimble in their ships and so well piloted into the Channel by English and Irish captives " that both the coasting trade and the fisheries of the district were held up, the seamen refusing to go to sea. It was not only interference with peaceful industry, however, that threw the West into a state occasion-ally bordering on panic : many hundreds of people had been for years deprived of bread-winners and relatives who were held to ransom in Algiers and other " *infami nidi di corsari*," as Tasso long before had characterised the coastline of the Barbary States. That the tables could sometimes

be turned upon the " Turks," despite the contemporary inefficiency of His Majesty's Fleet,
constitutes perhaps the chief interest of the
following tale.

When the people in the *Little David* were
disposed of at Sallee, it was the fate of John
Dunton to become the property of a Moorish
merchant named Aligolant, with whom he remained until 1636. Some time in August of that
year Aligolant was the predominant partner in a
venture for fitting out a ship to go to the English
Channel "for taking Englishwomen, being of
more worth than other," as Dunton in his de-
position puts it, speaking, no doubt, rather from
a knowledge of the Sallee market than from any
gallant or patriotic prejudice. One does not know
precisely how long this Englishman had been in
captivity, but two of the Dutchmen who sailed
with him in Aligolant's slave-trading bark had
been at Sallee over ten years ; and John may well
have had time enough there to win some measure
of his master's confidence. He, however, explains
his appointment as pilot of this piratical vessel as
a consequence of necessity, the worthy merchant
" having never a Christian slave but himself that
could take charge of a ship " : and we have
already seen that Christian slaves who had a
knowledge of navigation and of the English and
Irish Channels were often employed as pilots by
their masters. What strikes one as peculiar in
this case is that the ship should have been allowed
to sail with all her executive offices filled by men
of European birth. John Rickles, formerly of
Harling in Friesland, was made captain, and was

even permitted to have a sword, which the
Deputy-Governor of Hurst Castle (who presently
took it from him) considered to be worth at least
six pounds sterling of English money. Another
Dutchman, Jacob Cornelius, held the post of
gunner. Perhaps Aligolant and his brother specu-
lators argued that they might risk employing
the valuable skill and local knowledge of these
northern seamen because, after all, there were
but six of them all told—five of whom professed
to have renounced Christianity—against a Moorish
crew numbering twenty. It is at least certain
that the trustful owners did not know that
Rickles was already promising his compatriot,
Jacob Cornelius, whilst yet they talked together
on the harbour-side at Sallee, that he would
surely bring him back " into Christendom."

Early in September the bark, or caravel,
as it is indifferently called, was off the English
coast in apparent pursuance of her designs on
English womanhood. Dunton and the two principal Dutchmen had meanwhile worked out the
manner of their own enterprise. To the success
of this some reinforcement of their numbers was
clearly desirable. It was not long before an
English fishing-boat was descried ahead. She
was an unlikely craft to contain the kind of
merchandise in which Messrs. Aligolant and Co.
wished to deal, and moreover, in the opinion of
Mahomet and Hamet (as appeared by their
subsequent examinations) she was too close inshore to be safely pursued. But John Rickles,
sometime boatswain's mate of a good ship of
Hoorn, was at the helm, and he soon laid his

Moorish command alongside the fishing-boat, and added eight or nine lusty Englishmen to the European complement on board his vessel. Doubtless there was some fighting, as it would be impossible (with Mahomet and Hamet looking on) to explain at once to the astonished fishermen the part that it was hoped and expected they would play. One of them appears to have been drowned in the fracas, and upon that casualty was founded the allegation afterwards made of murder as well as of piracy upon the high seas. We may presume that to Dunton, as a compatriot, was entrusted the delicate business of making the captives aware that though the vessel in which they found themselves sailed under Moorish colours it was the captain's resolve, with their assistance, never to return to Sallee. Rickles afterwards stated that the men were captured " with intention to make a party against the Moors, according to a previous resolution of the rest of the Dutch and English on board " : and in some way or other, and as quickly as possible, the new-comers must have been informed of the plot. It was a safe communication, if adroitly made, for in the circumstances the fishermen had but a small chance of avoiding slavery in Algiers except by combining with the officers of this extraordinary ship against the crew— still the numerically superior party. It was a much more hopeful plan than to rely upon the possibility of recapture by any English man-of-war of those days.

Rickles did not wait long before he gave the signal for the Dutch and English " to stand up for their lives and liberties "; and upon their doing so with complete success, the Moors were driven below into the hold, and sail was made for the nearest land. As they came in at the Needles and approached Hurst Castle, they ran up a white flag and trailed the Turk's colours over the stern in the water in token of their friendly intentions. They were at once made prisoners.

The *coup* of these honest seamen was followed at once by bewildering legal complications, characteristic of the period. The surrender of the caravel to the Lieutenant-Governor of Hurst Castle inevitably led in those days to conflicting claims to her. Jerome, second Earl of Portland, who had lately been appointed Vice-Admiral of the coast for Hampshire, as soon as he heard of the affair sent his marshal to arrest the ship in the King's name. The Lieutenant-Governor of the Castle, Captain Barrett, acting on instructions from his superior, Edward, Lord Gorges, refused to deliver her, because a third party, Lord Arundel of Wardour, was already in the field and claimed her. This nobleman contended that the prize belonged to him under a grant by his late Majesty King James of the hundred of Westover and of all rights and perquisites thereunto belonging : but when Mr. Williams, the bailiff of the hundred of Westover would fain have arrested the ship, he too was refused possession upon similar grounds. There was also talk of a right of the town of Southampton to local admiralty *droits* extending as far away from that place as Hurst Castle. It is not surprising therefore, that Lord Gorges and his lieutenant held on to the prize pending instructions from the Council, then sitting at Windsor. The craft was said to be " of excellent sail " ; and ultimately orders came for her delivery to the officials in the Royal Dockyard at Portsmouth. Lord Gorges, however, still wanted to retain her powder and muskets, and Rickles' sea-chest and the good sword which had evidently caught his fancy : he also asked to be rewarded for " bringing in the bark," a service one would have imagined had been very satisfactorily accomplished by her own people. The multiplicity of jurisdictions here noted has disappeared : the view that a government should be bountiful for no particular reason is far less obsolete.

We are concerned, however, rather with the men than with the ship, which we may dismiss by saying that she disappointed the shipwrights at Portsmouth and was sold as unfit for adoption into His Majesty's Service. Hurst Castle allowed the English fishermen who had been picked up, and who had neither sea-chests nor swords to be coveted, to go to their homes, though some of them were afterwards brought back as witnesses : but the Moors and the Dutchmen and John Dunton were detained. It will be observed that only eleven Moors figure at the trial. Nothing appears regarding the fate of the other nine or ten originally on board. If these had been in the hold of the bark when she was brought in, they would certainly have appeared in the dock at Winchester : but an elementary knowledge of the ways of pirates enables us to surmise that some of the Moors were not driven into the hold, but went over the side, dead or alive, when Rickles gave the sign. There was reason enough for putting the Hollanders and Dunton on their trial along with the surviving Moors, since they had undoubtedly formed part of the corsair's complement, and it was fitting that their cases should be formally decided : but they were never in jeopardy and, indeed, some days before their trial were openly speaking of the reward that they too ought to receive from the Government for saving as many of His Majesty's subjects " as this bark would have been fraught withal "— that is to say, if the enterprise of Aligolant and partners had been successfully carried out. We do not hear what the Council thought of a claim based upon this hypothesis, but Dunton was ultimately rewarded, as we shall see, by being made useful to his country.

The High Court of Admiralty, which at this time sat in Southwark, was the proper tribunal to deal with the crime of piracy, but its judge, Sir Henry Marten, much alarmed for his own safety because of the prevalence of the plague in London, was just then before all things bent on relieving himself of his duties there by arranging makeshift trials of pirates in the country. With a show of independence not always observable in judges of the seventeenth century he had written to the Lords of the Admiralty in the previous June to say that if the parties and witnesses in a similar case that ought to have come up from Devon were brought to London it would not be the least good, as he should not be there ; he hoped " he should have liberty as other men had to secure his life by departing from that contagious place," and he suggested that the Vice-Admiralty Court at Plymouth might very well deal with the matter. In like manner the trial of these Moors was pushed into the un-accustomed hands of the Vice-Admiral of the Coast in Hampshire, though Sir Henry's letters written at this very time express the opinion that " most of the Vice-Admirals are ignorant " and that (presumably by way of cure) they ought to accustom themselves to the more frequent holding of criminal sessions. As they were not lawyers but administrative officials, and moreover could hardly have foreseen the appearance of the plague in London and its effect upon the per-sonnel of the High Court of Admiralty, one cannot blame them overmuch. Fortunately there was a tower of strength in the Registrar of the High Court, a certain Mr. Thomas Wyan, who was kept on the move instructing the provincial authorities how to conduct the trials of piratical persons. Marten had a high, and in the circum-stances, a convenient, opinion of this gentleman. He wrote to Mr. Secretary Nicholas that he was very expert and would be able " to direct the weakest Vice-Admiral or judge of admiralty." Indeed his reputation had reached the Vice-Admiral of Hampshire himself : the latter besought the Lords of Admiralty to command Mr. Wyan to be present at the trial at Winchester, although he, the Earl, had already a learned lawyer of Doctors' Commons, one Doctor Robert Mason, attached as judge to his vice-admiralty. Perhaps

c

both Portland and Dr. Mason were "weak" in Sir Henry Marten's sense. Certainly the Earl's legal terminology was colloquial rather than exact : he described the answers given by the Moors, after conviction, to the usual question why sentence of death should not be passed upon them as their "pleas." This, however, is slightly to anticipate the sequel : the important Mr. Wyan did come to the assistance of Dr. Mason, who also rode down from London to Winchester, and afterwards complained of the charges this and similar journeys had imposed upon him. He and his two men and three horses, he wrote, "cannot all feed upon hay and oats," and all the profits of his place amounted to but seven pounds a year. The manœuvres of Sir Henry Marten to get his London work done by others in the country certainly set one vice-admiralty judge talking about resigning his commission : but as yet Dr. Mason, unlike the judge of the High Court, could not avoid the discharge of his duties. We can only hope that the presence of the great and learned Registrar of the London Court at his elbow, ready to "direct" him, mitigated his sense of being victimised, and that he enjoyed the situation. Not every provincial judge would. Still, the prisoners had what Portland, the Vice-Admiral, considered "a very fair legal trial, with as good juries as have been seen here." The jury which dealt with the case with which we are concerned arrived at an easily foreseen verdict : the Moors were all convicted and the Dutchmen and John Dunton honourably acquitted. Not quite scatheless, however, emerged John Rickles and Jacob Cornelius and their fellow-countrymen, who, it will be remembered, had embraced Islam in captivity : for so eloquent was the judge's admonition to the renegades to repent of their apostasy that (according to the report of Mr. Wyan to the Secretary of the Admiralty) the captain fell down in a swoon through the sense of sin brought home to him, and was with difficulty restored.

It must not be imagined that the matter was now at an end, or that the final scene showed eleven corpses hanging in chains by the side of Portsmouth harbour. The Moors lay under sentence of death, but they were far too valuable to be executed : at least eleven Christian slaves in durance at Sallee could be exchanged for them. John Dunton had already put in a petition that one of them might be given to him wherewith to redeem his little son ; the fishermen had made similar requests, for they too had children or friends in the hands of the Moors. Needless to say the eleven convicts were themselves quite sure of the advantage to the English nation that would ensue from such an exchange : on the other hand the Dutch were afraid that if these Moors went back to Sallee and spread the story of how Aligolant had been cheated of ship and merchandise it would go hard with other Dutchmen out there. These were weighty matters, which the Lords of the Admiralty had to consider. Meanwhile there was the question of suitable rewards to the men who had brought in the ship. It was suggested that Rickles might be given a job as interpreter at a forthcoming piracy trial in Dorset—a benevolent if not an over-generous idea. Dunton upon his acquittal had come to London, where his story obtained for him the patronage of Sir Harry Vane. Lord Portland had already described him to the Lords of the Admiralty as " a lusty man," who might well be pressed for His Majesty's ships : and he was appointed master of the *Leopard*, the flagship of the squadron that under Captain William Rainsborough was at last despatched early in the following year against Sallee. Doubtless his knowledge of that hornet's nest was an additional recommendation, just as his acquaintance with the English Channel had induced his former employers, the Moors, to make him pilot. John launched out into authorship on the return of this expedition with a pamphlet entitled *A True Journal of the Sallee Fleet*, which work in gratitude and it may be, not unmindful of favours to come, he dedicated to Vane, whose influence had enabled him to accompany the expedition.

The Sallee Expeditionary Fleet and honest John Dunton had been gone a month and more, and still the Winchester convicts remained unhanged. In March two women whose husbands had been long prisoners in Algiers heard of these infidels, and successfully petitioned the Council that two of the prisoners might be delivered over to be exchanged. These things were urgent, since wives in the like situation were numerous, and were becoming a great charge upon the Poor-Law authorities of their several neighbourhoods. The order went forth : but unfortunately no Moors were to be found. With the consent of the Lords of the Admiralty an enterprising merchant had already taken the whole batch out of prison, covenanting to use them for the redemption of His Majesty's subjects. The financial details of this mysterious transaction are, of course, wanting, though it is not difficult to imagine that with the custody—one might almost say the ownership—of eleven Mussulmans so much in demand as pawns by grass-widows and others this engaging seventeenth-century profiteer would probably find himself in clover. We hear of an inquiry by the Council as to the name of the adventurer, but incredible as it sounds the Secretary to the Lords of the Admiralty, with whom the merchant had dealt, professed to be unable to give it. The story arising out of the voyage of Aligolant's caravel, ends as it began, with a commercial speculation.

III

THE BATTLE OF NEW BRIGHTON

THE beginning of the Seven Years' War found England quite unprepared. The right of the Crown to compel the service of the subject in a time of national emergency was being exercised in the year 1755 with a rigour that, given greater foresight, might not have been necessary. The contemporary prints are full of the doings of the Press-gang. The *Gentleman's Magazine* of May reports " the hottest press upon the Thames that has been since the warrants were granted," and says that it resulted (not without some infringement of protections and other illegalities) in the acquisition of a thousand men. Early in June the *Whitehall Evening Post* has a letter from Cornwall complaining of the brutalities of the impressment officers there ; and another evening paper tells a lurid story of a sailor who, having failed to bribe his captors, deliberately cut off one of his own fingers. " They write from Deal," says the *British Gazetteer* of the 14th June, " that the impressing for seamen is yet carried on there with much vigour, and that several have been taken out of homeward-bound ships arrived from foreign parts to hasten the equipping of our men-of-war." Perhaps even then newspapers were feeling their way towards headlines ; because,

dated in this very year, there is extant a letter
from Sir Thomas Salusbury, the Judge of the
Admiralty Court, addressed to the Secretary of
the Admiralty, informing him that he knows of
" several young fellows in the country who want
to join the Navy if he can recommend them to a
good captain." There is here, of course, the
whole difference between volunteering and compulsion, but the Judge's letter shows that the
Sea Service was less unpopular than we might
suppose, judging only from the printed sources;
though it may well be that Salusbury's young
fellows in the country knew very little about the
interior of a man-of-war of the period. The real
seaman knew a great deal, and what particularly
exasperated him was the pouncing upon him on
his return from a long foreign voyage, before
he could set his foot ashore. Outward-bound
ships were not molested, as that would have
interfered with the merchants' voyages; but all
round the coast during these months the press-
gang lay in wait for the returning mariner.

The fighting between the Navy and the Merchant Service which in consequence took place
at the mouth of the Mersey (not, by the way, the
only such encounter), has a tragi-comic character
in view of the half-hearted proceedings in the
High Court of Admiralty to which it led. Towards
the end of May, 1755, H.M.S. *Winchelsea*, of
twenty guns, Francis William Drake, Esq., Commander, was lying in the entrance to the estuary,
having orders from the Admiralty to impress
seamen, when an English merchant ship was
observed making for the river. She proved to

be the *Upton* of Liverpool, Thomas Birch, master, from Maryland. The *Winchelsea's* barge was sent to board the vessel, but found all her hands armed with muskets and cutlasses and her " great guns " loaded ; and the Navy boat was at once told to keep off or take her chance of being sunk. Birch, the skipper, diplomatically hailed the people in the barge from the *Upton's* cabin window, and said his seamen had " confined " him there and taken the command of the ship from him. The barge sheered off a little ; possibly Mr. Watson, the master's mate of the *Winchelsea*, who was in charge of the boat, was somewhat non-plussed. Meanwhile the crew of the *Upton* lowered their own boat and, rowing up to that of the man-of-war, swore that they would fire upon the men in her if they did not immediately go away, or if they attempted to hinder their landing ; " upon which," say the newspapers of the day, " a most bloody battle ensued." After the two boats had exchanged musketry fire, the merchant seamen made the mistake of attempting to board the barge, " sword in hand " ; but the Navy's men were too many for them, and drove them " upon the offside " of their boat, so that she " overset so far as to fill." Whereupon the un-lucky *Uptons*, who a short time before had declared they would die before they would be taken, surrendered to the number of fifteen, " choosing rather to be pressed than drowned." Probably the *Public Advertiser* of the 15th June is overstating the case when it says " several on both sides are mortally wounded " ; we hear nothing of this afterwards, when the facts were

laid before Counsel to advise what punitive steps
were to be taken. It is true that it appears by a
return made by Captain Drake of the *Winchelsea*
as to the disposal of the fifteen conscripts, that
one of them died before the month was out, but
he does not attribute it to the fighting. There
had, however, certainly been wounding on both
sides, and the reception of the fifteen on board
the man-of-war, whither they were at once
conveyed, may perhaps be imagined. This affair
of the *Upton* is, however, only connected with
the story we have to relate as a kind of prelude.

A few days later, the merchant ship *Tarleton*,
James Thompson, master, arrived off Liverpool.
She is variously described in the newspapers as
from Barbadoes and Guinea; perhaps she came
from both places, and by applying the doctrine
of continuous voyages backwards, a shrewd guess
may be hazarded at her trade. The same procedure was followed; the *Winchelsea's* victorious
barge, in charge this time of Lieutenant Gideon,
was sent to meet her " being then under sail to
come round the Rock of Liverpool." Again
when the barge came alongside she found a
ship's crew armed with blunderbusses, pistols
and cutlasses, and one of the ship's guns loaded
with grape; and was once more warned in
appropriately forcible language, to keep off or be
sunk. Lieutenant Gideon repeatedly asked for
the captain, but that officer appeared to have
retired to his cabin as Mr. Birch, the master of
the *Upton*, had done. The person who pretended
to be the captain was really James Berry, the
carpenter, and he " in a contemptuous manner

waved his hat at the barge and with his crew gave shouts and cheers or halloas which was [*sic*] attended with many curses and wicked oaths and threats that they would cut any person in pieces who should board them." It is strange that at such a juncture Lieutenant Gideon should have stickled for form ; even amidst these wicked jeers he calmly asked whether they would not pay some respect to His Majesty's colours by showing those of the *Tarleton* and lowering their top-gallant sail. There seems to have been something a little theatrical about Gideon ; in the affidavit he made a few days later before the Mayor of Liverpool, describing what had taken place, he says that when the sailors refused to strike their top-gallant sail he himself fired a musket ball through the canvas that remained so improperly immovable. It is difficult to find a reason for this piece of bravado. If by some extraordinary chance he had cut the halyard and brought the sail down, it might have made the *Tarleton* look nicer from the point of view of naval etiquette, but it seems to have escaped this zealous officer that the essence of the matter was that she should lower it herself. At any rate, there was now no chance of her doing so with her crew on deck firing muskets at the man-of-war's boat. And though a volley is spoken of, it is only alleged that several of the shot fell near the barge and one of them struck the barge's stern-post. Possibly anger impaired the men's marksmanship ; possibly the barge was not particularly close ; the *Advertiser*, indeed, unkindly suggests that the fight with the

Upton had not been without its effect, and at
any rate one can well imagine that the whole
business was little calculated to arouse enthusiasm.
Lieutenant Gideon, however, returned the fire,
also quite harmlessly ; and he then rowed back
to the *Winchelsea* to acquaint Captain Drake
with what had happened. He appears to have
suggested to Drake that the *Winchelsea* would
have an opportunity of firing upon the *Tarleton*
as she passed by, coming up the river. This was
accordingly done, without damage, but also without acknowledgment by way of salute. Presumably, though it is not so stated, the *Winchelsea*
was at anchor. Her barge followed the *Tarleton*
up the river at a respectful distance, near enough
however to hear her crew " desiring one another
to mind their aim " as they fired their muskets.
And when the *Tarleton* came opposite the town
of Liverpool, her crew " ran her into the dock,
and all made their escape from her, by means
of which not one of them could be impressed
into His Majesty's Service."

The similarity of the two merchant captains'
behaviour in repudiating responsibility for the attitude of their respective crews is probably the first
point that will strike the reader of this narrative.
It is possible that the *Tarleton*, which only the day
before the encounter had taken a pilot on board,
" to bring the vessel round the Rock," had full
particulars of the *Upton* affair from him. He
would probably be full of it. As an official person
with a reputation to keep up, he had (he afterwards
said) been scandalised by the *Tarleton's* conduct ;
and whilst on board had proposed to lay the

Tarleton's topsail aback when the *Winchelsea*
fired at her in passing. But he only received a
curse and a blow with the flat of a cutlass for his
punctilio. If such was his disposition, it is likely
enough that he had acquainted Mr. Thompson
with the neutral attitude taken up by Mr. Birch
of the *Upton*, a day or two before. It may be
also that the determination of the two skippers
to stand aside and let their men do what they
could to escape illustrates the beginning of what
later became an acknowledged practice. The
stories of Captain Marryat are still useful in
throwing light upon the sea customs of his day,
and there is an episode in the *Adventures of Mr.
Midshipman Easy* similar to, if less Homeric than,
the conflict we have been describing. The
novelist's opinion of the usual and proper attitude
for the merchant captain to adopt on such occasions is expressed through the mouth of Mr.
Oxbelly : " That the men have a right to resist
if possible," says Mr. Oxbelly, " is admitted ;
they always do so and never are punished for
so doing. Under the guns of the frigate, of
course, we should only have to submit ; but
those two boats do not contain more than twenty-
five men, I should think, and our men are the
stronger party. We had better leave it to them
and stand neuter." But that this opinion was
by no means settled in 1755 will appear from the
sequel.

The proceedings at law began by the swearing
of detailed affidavits before the Mayor of Liverpool by the punctilious pilot, the histrionic
Lieutenant Gideon and the Master's Mate and a

midshipman from the *Winchelsea*. The case of
the *Tarleton* was apparently regarded as the more
serious one of the two because there the *Winchelsea's* endeavour had been completely frus-
trated. The whole crew, including Berry the
carpenter, had escaped. There remained Mr.
Thompson, the master, not himself in virtue of
his rank liable to impressment, but who had by
the temporary abdication of his command con-
nived at the conduct of his men. The affidavits
were sent in due course to Mr. Crespigny, the
Admiralty Proctor in London; and on the
24th June the Judge of the Admiralty Court,
having heard them read, decreed that a warrant
should issue against Thompson and Berry. The
warrant which is dated a few days later calls upon
the defendants to answer " for an insult shown to
His Majesty's colours, and for opposing and
preventing His Majesty's ship the *Winchelsea's*
boat coming on board the ship *Tarleton* and for
firing from the ship on the said boat and thereby
wounding several of His Majesty's subjects in
contempt of His Majesty's authority." This was
all very well, but Thompson's " opposition " had
consisted merely in lying low and saying nothing,
and the insulting Berry, who had directed the
firing, was nowhere to be found. Somebody,
however, seems to have thought of Lieutenant
Gideon's curiously timed demand for a salute;
it might be possible to corner Mr. Thompson, as
indubitably the master of the ship, upon that
point. There was an old Admiralty regulation
to the effect that " if any of His Majesty's subjects
shall so far forget their duty as to attempt to pass

any of His Majesty's ships without striking their topsails " certain penal consequences should ensue. The practice is of course to be distinguished from the salute exacted through several centuries from the foreigner—even though he might be a man-of-war—when he met our Navy whilst navigating " the British seas." It rather concerns the respect due from the uncommissioned to a King's ship—from the one Service to the other—which had over it an implied and in some matters even a statutory superintendence. It was a purely municipal regulation, the omission to comply with which was the subject of a prosecution as late as the year 1829. It is to be remembered also that the Admiralty Court, in the middle of the eighteenth century, was little more than a department of the Admiralty. The salary of the Judge was provided for in the ordinary annual estimate for the Navy : amongst the duties of the Marshal of the Court and his subordinates were the pursuit and apprehension of deserters from the Fleet, and upon occasion even the custody of naval officers awaiting trial by court-martial. At a period when assisting in these ways the maintenance of military discipline within the Royal Navy was included in the duties of the Admiralty Court officials, the lawyers at Doctors' Commons had probably as strong views on the propriety of salutes by merchantmen as any flag-officer in Whitehall. If in the present case the salute could have hardly been expected at the precise moment when Lieutenant Gideon shot at the *Tarleton's* topsail from his barge, it was undeniable that a little later the merchantman had passed the *Winchelsea*

at anchor without taking the slightest notice of
her. The case was accordingly laid before Doctors
Hay and Pinfold of Doctors' Commons, who were
respectively King's Advocate and Admiralty Advocate at the time, and on the 17th July they gave
it as their opinion "that the *Tarleton*, by refusing
to lower their top-gallant sail, are guilty of an
offence cognisable in the Court of the Admiralty
and punishable at the discretion of the Judge."
The grammar of this sentence is curious and the
master's name is not mentioned. But Thompson
was in fact arrested. Nothing more occurred for
some time, but in November two London merchants who knew Thompson and probably required his services as a navigator, became bail
for him in the sum of £200 and he was released.
Thenceforward the case of "Our Sovereign Lord
the King in his Office of Admiralty against James
Thompson, now or late master of the ship called
the *Tarleton*," makes periodical appearances in
the records of the Admiralty Court and is as
often adjourned. Mr. Crespigny, the Proctor,
was never ready to go on, though an interesting
argument as to the responsibility of Captain
Thompson, snugly ensconced in his cabin, for
what was taking place on deck waited to be
unfolded. He, good man, had presumably his
living to earn and was doubtless long ago at sea
again. In fact, the atmosphere of Doctors'
Commons, in the dining-room of which the Court
was frequently held, was one of cloistered leisure.
It does not appear that Mr. Crespigny was even
reproved for his dilatoriness. The Judge, Sir
Thomas Salusbury, a man of ample wealth, had

his country seat far away in Hertfordshire ; we find Dr. Ducarel, a learned antiquary, sitting in court for him in July and again in September. It was not until the end of April, 1757, nearly two years after the offence, that Crespigny came one morning into Court, and announced that he had " orders "—the word is to be noted—not to prosecute further, if the other side would pay the expenses. Perhaps the London merchants came to the rescue again ; at any rate, the expenses were paid, and the Judge, by a decree which in the circumstances is rather quaintly styled " interlocutory," dismissed the bail.

Parturiunt montes, no doubt : but the case seems worth notice as showing the process of the Admiralty Court employed for an end now long obsolete.

IV

ABOUT nine o'clock one calm Sunday morning in August, 1802, the longshoremen of Brighton were surprised to see a small brig some three or four miles away flying a signal of distress. She was seen to be gradually settling down, and several boats and a revenue cutter called the *Swallow* at once put out to her. They found the crew already in the ship's boat waiting for the captain and mate, who were still on board. The captain waved the rescuers off, although the brig was already on her beam ends, saying that she was his as long as she could swim. Notwithstanding this strange behaviour, the *Swallow* made a rope fast to the ship with the intention of towing her into shallower water. Almost immediately afterwards, however, she went down.

She was the *Adventure* of London, William Codlin, master, ostensibly bound to the Mediterranean, and said to contain a very valuable cargo. She sank in six fathoms of water, and it was remarked at the time by those conversant with the coast that after making her signal she seemed to seek a deeper place to sink in—or at least made no attempt to come nearer to the beach.

The boatmen of Brighton were resourceful, and they succeeded in sweeping two hawsers

D

under her at low tide, and so lifting her : and by the following Thursday morning, the weather favouring their exertions, the *Adventure* had been gradually brought close inshore. Subsequently they took her into Shoreham Harbour. But before this could be done it was necessary to plug up certain holes in her planking, just below the level of the cabin floor, from which apertures the tell-tale water came running out when she was beached. The holes had been made unmistakably from within.

The chief interest of this story of a bungled crime—apart from its rather pretty irony—lies in the illustration it affords of the trickishness of the criminal law at the time : and, in fact, it gave rise, a little later, to remedial legislation. The two London merchants, Easterby and Macfarlane, who planned the loss of their own ship, and who, so far as appears, were alone to profit by it, got off without legal punishment. Codlin was their catspaw. Paragraphs in the contemporary press which followed upon his execution describe him as one of the best seamen in the North Coast trade : and suspicious as are such sources of eulogy it is clear that as a fraudulent scuttler of ships he was at any rate a mere tyro. His employer, Mr. Easterby, coming down to Brighton, when the news of the " accident " reached him, called Codlin a damned fool. It is possible that even a person with no interest in the result would have summed up the Captain's mismanagement of the part allotted to him on this occasion in very similar terms. The explanation why so good a North-country sailorman undertook to play it at all is perhaps to be found in the sentence with which the *Naval Chronicle* closes its account of the affair. Codlin was out of employment and his wife and children were in distress at the time he entered into the fatal plot with the owners.

The *Adventure* was a clinker-built little vessel of 77 tons, described in her certificate as a " square sterned brigantine " built at Exmouth in 1797, and had been purchased by Easterby and Macfarlane in June, 1802. They effected insurances upon her amounting in the whole to £700, and the cargo with which they proceeded to load her and which was insured for nearly £10,000 included, according to them, sixty pieces of silver plate, china, cutlery, wearing apparel and a grand piano. Then there was a meeting at Easterby's house at Rotherhithe, when he and his partner were present, together with Codlin, lately appointed master of their new ship, and a man named Sharrow, who was to sail in her as supercargo. Easterby remarked, apparently *à propos de bottes*, that many ships had been sunk to take in the underwriters, and he supposed would be again. Macfarlane echoed the remark, and the two shipowners looked across at Codlin, who said he supposed so too. By the next time they met, a few days before the ship sailed, Easterby seems to have completed his sounding of the captain, and to have evolved a definite scheme. It was then proposed that the ship should proceed to Gibraltar and the cargo be there sold : that afterwards an opportunity should be taken to sink her, the people on board escaping in the boat ; and that

it should be represented to the underwriters that
only half of the cargo had been disposed of and
that the other half had gone down with the ship.
This programme was subsequently divulged by
Sharrow to show what manner of men Easterby
and Macfarlane were ; but there is evidence that
it was abandoned by those gentlemen in favour
of the shorter way of sinking the brig in the
Channel—though hardly within view of the English coast at nine o'clock on a fine morning.
In fact, a considerable number of packages was
taken out of the *Adventure* before she left the
Thames and concealed—some in Easterby's house,
some in Macfarlane's, and some by a lady friend
of Macfarlane's, one Mrs. Phyllis Patterson, who
was kind enough to find house-room for part of
them. That a less lengthy voyage than had been
originally contemplated was finally decided upon
seems clear, because a quantity of the *Adventure's*
own stores—also covered by insurance—was
quietly transferred to the *William*, another of
the firm's ships in the Thames. It is significant
also that when the *Adventure* left London she went
first to Yarmouth and there took in fifteen tons
of ballast, and (as an extra hand) a bricklayer's
labourer.

From Yarmouth she sailed to the Downs, and
at Deal the mate, Mr. Douglas, found that his
rheumatism would not allow him to proceed
further and both he and the Mr. Sharrow already
mentioned left the ship. Sharrow, at any rate,
knew what was in the wind and thought better
of it in time. Cooper, a seaman who had joined
at Limehouse, was thereupon appointed mate

in the place of Douglas. He was honest enough to explain that he had no knowledge of navigation and had never sailed as mate, but Codlin, equally frank, told him it did not matter in the least as he would not be forty-eight hours longer on board. A new supercargo named Reid was shipped, and the *Adventure* left Deal on the Friday before the eventful Sunday, carrying six persons, Codlin the master, Cooper the newly promoted mate, James Welch the bricklayer, Reid, and a couple of boys. As they set sail the Captain gave strict orders that nothing was to be put in the boat except the four oars : in those days the boat, carried inboard in the waist of the ship, would in an ordinary way have been made into a receptacle for everything about the deck that could be stowed in it.

On Saturday night Codlin told Cooper to take up a hatch in the cabin floor and bore three holes as low down in the run as possible with some new augurs he would find there. The augurs were left in the holes overnight, and the cabin boy was forbidden to come down into the cabin to set out the breakfast. On Sunday morning the augurs were pulled out, but the water came in very slowly, and a crowbar was found necessary to make a really effective hole.

The careful Codlin got everybody but himself and Cooper into the boat before the water was up to the cabin floor. His signal of distress was pathetically premature. By taking three hours to sink the *Adventure* seriously embarrassed him ; she should have been at the bottom before the boats which put out from the shore reached the spot. His momentary attitude of a defensive character with regard to them seems to show that he had quite lost his head. They were unwelcome, but they were not wreckers.

Two days afterwards—on the Tuesday, Messrs. Easterby and Macfarlane boldly gave notice of abandonment of the cargo to the underwriters; but with the discovery on Thursday of the holes in the ship's planking, obviously made from inside, the game was up. The *Adventure*, almost a new ship, was in every respect quite seaworthy. There was found in her at Shoreham neither silver plate nor grand piano, but that was scarcely odd because those valuable goods had probably never been in anything more nautical than a bill of lading. The original value of the cargo found on board her was estimated when undamaged to have been about three pounds. Brighton became too hot for the conspirators, and Macfarlane booked places in the London coach for Codlin and Cooper, bidding them take a humble lodging at the journey's end and lie low. But upon a reward for information leading to their discovery being advertised some friends of Cooper's offered to deliver him up on condition that he was admitted as King's evidence. His own account was that going down into the country to see his mother at Saxmundham he at once surrendered to the village constable on hearing that he was wanted. At any rate, he told what he knew of the story before the Lord Mayor at the Mansion House. Codlin was caught off Harwich, already some way out in the continental packet.

Easterby and Macfarlane having been also

arrested were tried, along with their underlings,
Codlin and Reid, on the 26th of October following,
at the Admiralty Sessions at the Old Bailey
before Lord Chief Justice Ellenborough, in the
presence of Sir W. Scott, the judge of the Admiralty
Court. There was little against Reid. He had
indeed slept in the cabin throughout the business
with the augurs and the crowbar : but he was
proved to be deaf and was acquitted. The jury
found the three others guilty of felony. The great
Erskine had been briefed to defend Easterby,
and he raised the point that as no act had been
done by the owners within the jurisdiction of
the Admiralty Court they could not properly be
convicted before it. Put shortly, that meant
there was no evidence that either Easterby or
Macfarlane had ever been on board the *Adventure*
upon the high seas : though the former as super-
intendent of the operations, was certainly at
Deal when she touched there, and when probably
the plan of campaign was altered. The point
was argued before the full bench of twelve judges
on two occasions in November, first in the Exchequer Chamber and subsequently at Serjeant's
Inn, and so great was the crowd outside the
Hall of the latter place that even those who had
business there could scarcely gain admittance.
The public interest in a dry point of law can only
be accounted for by the existence of widespread
indignation at the loophole afforded by it to the
principal culprits. Erskine himself was apologetic,
remarking that he represented the law and must
not be taken to be palliating the offence of which
his clients had been found guilty. The Judges

took time to consider. Meanwhile the misguided mariner, Codlin, whose futile iniquities
were clearly within the jurisdiction of the
Admiralty Court, was duly hanged, the procession
escorting him from Newgate to Execution Dock
headed, as the custom was, by the Deputy Marshal
of the Admiralty Court mounted on horseback
and bearing his silver oar. On the 2nd February,
1803, the Judges unanimously decided in favour
of Erskine's contention : and Messrs. Easterby
and Macfarlane subsequently received a free
pardon.

Erskine's point was successful, but it was
hardly what in these days would be called a
" brain-wave." It had always been raised when-
ever it could be. Fifty years earlier the same
objection had been taken on behalf of a prisoner
in a similar case—one Thomas Pow, who without
once going near the sea had made all arrangements
for the destruction of the brig *Nightingale* by fire
in the Bristol Channel. But it was left undecided
whether or not Pow's doings were properly
within the Admiralty jurisdiction because he was
able to escape by a different loophole the felon's
death that duly overtook his minion, the master
of the *Nightingale*. He happened to be a tailor
by trade, and though on this occasion he had
acted as a kind of shipping agent, he could not
be shown to be either an " owner, master, captain,
officer or mariner " of the brig, and it was against
such persons alone that the statute under which he
was indicted was directed. But the pleasant
quillet about jurisdiction cropped up again in
1785 upon the trial of a man named Coombes

charged with abetting the murder of Mr. William Allen, the Master of H.M.S. *Orestes*. There had been what amounted to a small battle in Christchurch Harbour between a large party of smugglers and their sympathisers on the one hand, and the boats of the *Orestes* on the other. The latter, coming in from seaward with the intention of seizing the smugglers' luggers which were in the harbour, were subjected for nearly three hours to a desultory musketry fire by the lawbreakers, and there was no doubt that Coombes was amongst the firing-party on shore. One of the boats grounded upon a sandbank, and Allen, at the moment when he was struck by the bullet that mortally wounded him, was standing in the water trying to shove her off. The prisoner Coombes was defended by Mr. Fielding, the son of the novelist, and by Mr. Garrow, afterwards a famous advocate and a Baron of the Court of Exchequer, though at this date a young man of but some two years' standing at the Bar. These gentlemen promptly raised the question whether, since the deceased when he was hit, was standing upon what a contemporary narrative quaintly calls a "hilly" part of the harbour, and the shot came from the land, the murder could be said to have been done upon the high seas—that is to say, within the jurisdiction of the Admiralty as charged in the indictment. Ought not Coombes to have been tried at the Assizes for the county? The point was again argued on two occasions before the judges, but beyond prolonging Coombes' sojourn in the condemned cell for six months it availed him nothing. But it was well known, and is typical of the technicalities of the criminal law in the eighteenth century.

To return in conclusion to the felonious scuttling of ships, there is, of course, observable (until they came to be built of iron) a natural sameness in the methods of the malefactors. The piece of perforated planking produced in court figures in later cases than that which we have been considering. What is more curious is the recurrence of the pretence of a foreign voyage, followed by the hasty sinking of the ship when only, as it were, just round the corner from her port of departure. " If 'twere done, 'twere well it were done quickly " seems to have occurred to more than one misguided seaman. It is the reflection of one who mislikes the task he has undertaken.

V

NEPTUNE AS DEFENDANT

"AT sea they have a ridiculous ceremony,"
wrote the Sieur Guillet de Saint George
in the year 1678—" prophane et ridicule " are the
words in the original—" that when Sailors cross
the Line or Tropic that have not been there before
they must pay certain forfeitures demanded of
them or else be ducked or baptised (as they call
it) either from the main yard-arm or otherwise "
—adding that each nation making voyages to the
East had a different form of initiation. Ducking
" the baptised " from the main-yard must have
been the most drastic form—" as if he were a
criminal," as Esquemeling, writing about the
same time of Dutch methods, had observed.
Other commentators, such as Osbeck, merely
mention that the men having been called on
deck, pails of water were thrown over those who
had not crossed the line before—a variant so
pleasant under the Equator that those who were
exempt by the rules of the game often, he says,
voluntarily " partook of the bathing." There
were doubtless also seamen who enjoyed,
even as victims, the rough-and-tumble described
by Falconer, the dressing up as Neptune and
Amphitrite, and the shaving and ducking which
came to be practised in English ships, as every
schoolboy has heard. But when Neptune laid

hands on passengers it happened once or twice that they were so deficient in the saving grace of humour as to take legal proceedings as soon as they got ashore. I have not found any record of such a case having been tried in England, but separated by an interval of fifty years, there were two in India, and perhaps the uncommon nature of such an action at law may justify a brief recital of the facts in those forgotten suits.

Mr. Nathaniel Castleton Maw was a young man who, having obtained a cadetship in the military service of the East India Company, was in 1801 proceeding to Bombay to commence his duties. The ship in which he sailed together with some seven or eight other young gentlemen destined for the same profession was called the *Scaleby Castle* : and when she was nearing the line the sailors in accordance with custom announced that the passengers would be expected to undergo the ceremony of shaving and ducking at the hands of Father Neptune. Mr. Maw from the first declared that he would not submit to it : the others were disposed to treat the matter as a joke, though that was before they knew how far it would be carried. There was a particular reason why Maw should have an objection to horseplay of the kind usual on such occasions since he was afflicted with a withered arm or some deformity of the kind. It could hardly have been of a serious nature or it would have stood in the way of his soldiering, and as a matter of fact he was made a lieutenant before 1802. But however slight his infirmity it was natural that he should shrink from anything likely to call public attention to it. Besides this private reason another and a more general one was stated to have weighed with him in resisting from the outset the threatened attack upon his dignity. With the exception of the few British seamen who were intent upon the accustomed ceremonial the whole of the crew were natives of India, and Mr. Maw thought that the spectacle of an English officer being shaved and ducked by the forecastle would be liable to be misunderstood by Orientals.

Now it was usually a pleasing feature of the shaving and ducking rite that exemption might be purchased for a pecuniary or a spirituous consideration—possibly always much the same thing : at all events the English practice so far as I am aware shows nothing similar to the pious use mentioned by Osbeck of devoting a portion of the " collection " on these occasions to " the Orphan House at Gothenburgh." Mr. Maw offered to pay the customary tax and one can only suppose that he must either by excess of dignity or angry words have rendered himself so obnoxious to the crew that they put him, so to speak, out of court. Certain it is that on the morning of the 28th September, when the line was crossed, Maw was walking about the deck armed with a cutlass and pistols and breathing defiance : and this notwithstanding that the Captain had given notice that any passenger who disliked the impending pastimes of the crew might retire into his (the Captain's) cabin. It is not clear why Maw did not do so, and without in the least excusing the violence to which he was subjected one can see that a different demeanour on his part might probably have avoided the whole affair.

Perhaps he took a youthful pride in tilting at established custom, though it is impossible now to say exactly how the matter came to a head ; but after the display of the cutlass and the touch-me-who-dare attitude, further offers of liquor to be supplied on arrival at Bombay, even when backed by the surety-ship of Mr. Patterson, the fourth officer, were of no avail. Father Neptune was evidently roused and determined to vindicate his importance, for Mr. Learmouth, the first officer, when Maw asked if he might go into his own cabin during the ceremony, told him that he would not be safe there. Maw, however, went, barricaded the door with boxes and trunks, and even took care to close his port to prevent invasion from without. But the stubbornness which led him thus to deprive himself of light and air in a stuffy cabin under the Line during the hottest part of the day was matched by that of the other side. Learmouth was right, and Raymond, the third mate, now gave countenance to the proceedings of the crew, and suggested, if he did not actually direct, that the door should be forced and the port opened. Maw does not seem to have known how to fasten the latter properly : and whilst one contingent of Neptune's party took the carpenter below to unscrew the hinges from the door, a seaman named Edwards was let down the ship's side to negotiate the port. This worthy, who had a drawn cutlass in one hand, succeeded in lifting up the port to a certain extent with a stick which he carried in the other, and he

proceeded to make thrusts with the more lethal
weapon through the aperture. Mr. Maw was
probably not placed in much jeopardy thereby,
and his military instinct no doubt rejoiced in the
clash of steel upon steel as he 'parried with his
sword. How long Edwards, precariously thrusting
from outside, and Mr. Maw, fencing in the semi-
darkness inside, continued this comical combat
does not appear : but the former bore in mind
the superior armament of Mr. Maw in having
two pistols and did not venture further through
the port-hole until he heard them fired off. Then
he leapt into the cabin at the same moment as
the other myrmidons of the sea-god burst open
the door. Apparently they had all been waiting
for the pistols to go off, not aware that Mr. Maw
with a restraint and care for theatrical effect
alike creditable to him had only loaded them
with powder. Once Mr. Maw's barriers were
down he was an easy victim and quickly dis-
armed of his cutlass. His assailants then dragged
him up on deck, where he managed for some
time to delay his execution by hanging on to the
door-post of the cuddy, calling out lustily meanwhile for the Captain. That officer, however,
remained discreetly in his cabin during the whole
performance and afterwards professed to have
heard nothing either of the shouts or of the
struggle. Messrs. Learmouth and Raymond, the
first and third officers, were on deck, but so far
from interfering with Maw's tormentors, con-
siderately took care of his watch for him. He was
at length torn from his hold, and in spite of all
his attempts to escape—his advocate in the

action for assault subsequently brought gravely
stated that at this juncture his client tried to
jump overboard—was taken along the quarter-
deck to the waist and forcibly held down in a boat
placed there half-full of dirty water for the
business of the day. His eyes were bandaged
with something not too clean, tar was rubbed
upon his face and scraped off again with the
usual piece of rusty hoop-iron, and he was duly
ducked in the dirty water, all in the most orthodox
fashion.

Mr. Maw brought his action of assault and
battery against Learmouth and Raymond, joining
as defendants a number of the seamen, members
of Neptune's gang, whom one would have thought
hardly worth legal powder and shot. The case
was tried in March, 1802, in the Recorder's Court
at Bombay. It was not alleged that the plaintiff
had been in any way differently treated from the
other six or seven young gentlemen, except in
so far as he had himself accentuated matters by
refusing to " come quietly." But consent being
of course the crux of the whole matter it could
not be denied that a violent assault had been
made upon him. The sea custom was merely
mentioned by the defence as some palliation of
what had occurred, and it is of interest to note
that in 1802 it was stated to have been " put a
stop to from a sense of its impropriety in nine
ships out of ten." It is rather surprising that
Captain Gardiner of the *Scaleby Castle* was
allowed to escape responsibility for what was
going on in his own ship by simply remaining
below. He was called as a witness to testify to

the impropriety of the plaintiff's treatment and was permitted to say that he (the Captain) would not have allowed it had he been present, but he was not made a defendant, and the Judge at the hearing contented himself with the mild observation that he wished Gardiner had been on deck. The responsibility of the first and third officers was patent : they were in charge of the deck the whole time, and according to one witness Learmouth had himself thrown a bucket of water over the plaintiff. Thus encouraged by their officers not very much blame perhaps attached to the seamen : and the 400 rupees, which were awarded as damages against all the defendants generally, were no doubt levied against Messrs. Learmouth and Raymond, as the Recorder suggested.

In the later case—or rather cases—heard in the Small Cause Court at Madras in September, 1851, the Captain and First Officer of the *True Briton* were separately sued by a passenger named King, a ship's steward, who had been lathered with a mixture of flour and water and well drenched in salt water in a " crossing the line " diversion on board that ship. Some week or two before the hearing twelve saloon passengers advertised in the *Madras Spectator* a testimonial to Captain Roe's " unremitting endeavours " to promote their comfort during the voyage, and signified their intention to present him with a piece of plate. Whether this public eulogium had any effect or not, or whether King's excitable behaviour—he was said to have broken the cuddy window in revenge—told against him, the

E

court was evidently reluctant to mulct the Captain in damages. But the Judge was obliged to lay it down that passengers were entitled to the protection of the Captain, whom he described as a magistrate on board. The case of Maw against Learmouth was cited, being apparently the only known precedent, but it was distinguished from the case then before the court inasmuch as King had not sought the protection of the officers as Maw had done in vain. A suggested arrangement between the parties coming to nothing, R.100 damages were awarded. Then immediately afterwards the claim against the First Officer was called on and the point was raised (by the same advocate who had defended the Captain) that it could not be proved that this defendant resided within the jurisdiction of the Court. This technical contention was upheld, the Judge remarking that had the objection been taken in Captain Roe's case he would have decided it in his favour. Truly the course of justice in the Small Cause Court of Madras seems that day to have zig-zagged a little; but if Captain Roe had to pay his R.100 it is to be hoped that his piece of plate " with a suitable inscription " more than compensated him.

The above stories are abridged from the Indian newspapers respectively reporting them. Incidentally they raise the question of the nature and extent of the authority of the merchant skipper over the people in his ship, both passengers and crew. At law his position has been left very vague: yet, as Lindsay, the historian of our merchant shipping puts it, " a ship at sea

is in herself a little kingdom," and some measure
of disciplinary power over the people on board
must needs be conceded even to the uncommissioned officer in command. Long ago the
jealousy of the commissioned officers of the
King's ships tended to keep obscure the authority
of their mercantile brethren : in the *Six Dialogues
about Sea Services*, which a certain Captain
Boteler published towards the end of the seventeenth century, it is complained with great
hauteur that masters of merchant ships are
actually " taking upon them the Titles of Captains." But the chief reason for saying as little
as possible about the master-mariner's authority
—and that only when occasion makes it unavoidable—has been the law's regard for the liberty
of the subject : and when an occasion does arise
for disciplinary measures they are subsequently
justified, if questioned, only by showing them
to have been necessary for the safety of the ship
and those on board.

There was a curious case in 1805 in which a
Mr. Boyce, a passenger on board the *Huddart*,
East Indiaman, brought an action against the
captain for assault and false imprisonment. One
evening in May of that year, the *Huddart*, being
then near the Cape of Good Hope in the course
of her voyage from Bombay to London, descried
two strange sail in the offing, which were supposed
to be enemies. The captain immediately mustered all hands, including the passengers, and
assigned to everyone his station for the defence
of the ship should a capture be attempted by the
strangers. He ordered Boyce along with the

other passengers to take up positions on the
poop, where they were to fight with small arms.
Everyone obeyed except only the plaintiff, whose
feelings had been hurt on some previous occasion
because the captain had forbidden him to take
the air in that particular part of the ship. He
was willing to fight anywhere else, but not on
the poop. This childishness was met by an order
to carry Mr. Boyce thither, and then unfortunately the irate captain went too far and secured
the presence of the plaintiff at his post during
the whole of the ensuing night by clapping him
in irons. The next morning the supposed enemy
ships had vanished, and the *Huddart* soon afterwards arrived safely at St. Helena. There the
indignant Mr. Boyce left the ship, and got a
passage home to England in another one. At
the trial of the action, in which the plaintiff
recovered damages, Lord Ellenborough said that
on the approach of an enemy the captain had
authority to do all that was necessary for the
safety of those on board, and had a right to assign
to each of them a station which it was his duty to
accept. What further rights the captain had in
case a passenger took a different view was a
topic left, as usual in these discussions, con-
veniently in the air—except as regards the use
of bilboes.

VI

ROBERT JEFFERY was eighteen years old
on the 11th December, 1807, and was
described, a year or two afterwards, when he was
temporarily famous, as a weakly-looking youth
of spare build and fair complexion. He was, in
1807, serving as an ordinary seaman on board
H.M.S. *Recruit*, commanded by Captain the Hon.
Warwick Lake on the West Indian Station.
Ashore he had been a smith or farrier, and however he may have made his entry into the Service
he was anything but a success as a sailor. He was
regarded in the *Recruit* as a skulker, and, moreover, he had been flogged in November for stealing
a bottle of rum out of the gunner's cabin. And
now on the 13th of December he was accused of
broaching a cask of spruce beer, a crime of which
he may or may not have been guilty. He was
never put upon his trial for it.

On the evening of that day the *Recruit* was
close to Sombrero, a small island of the Leeward
Group, some mile and a half in circumference,
and about twenty-five north-westward of Anguilla.
It was at that date uninhabited. Dusk was
coming on, but there was still light enough to
have seen houses or other signs of habitation if
there had been any. The sea around was empty
of vessels other than the *Recruit*. Her captain

came on deck at this time and, addressing Spencer, the Master, said, " Have we not some thieves on board ? " That officer replied, " Yes, there are two who have been guilty of theft." The captain then said, " Send up Jeffery here. I will not keep such a fellow in my ship," and a serjeant of marines was sent below for him. It appears that Spencer had on some previous occasion said to the captain that it would be a good thing if they could get Jeffery out of the ship.

The captain next ordered a painter to paint the word " Thief " on a piece of canvas, and upon Jeffery being brought up from below the patch was sewn upon his back. He was then bundled into a boat in charge of the lieutenant, Mr. Mould. There were neither water nor provisions in the boat, nor had the unfortunate seaman any clothes but those he stood up in. His clothes seem to have been brought on deck, but the Captain said, " Never mind his things," as the boat shoved off. One of the boat's crew gave him a pair of shoes, another a knife, and Mould presented him with a handkerchief, not so much to wear as to enable him to attract attention by waving it. The Lieutenant, at any rate, seems to have had small belief in the existence of Sombrero's inhabitants. It was dark when the boat returned to the ship, leaving Jeffery behind. The *Recruit* was still within sight of the island next morning, with a fair wind to reach it, but neither Spencer nor Mould nor any of the officers suggested to the Captain that Jeffery should be fetched off : and the ship sailed away. Giving his evidence afterwards the serjeant of marines deposed that the men round about him were saying when the boat was going away with Jeffery that he would be starved to death ; but upon Mr. Spencer coming up behind them and observing, " You be damned," he was for his own part immediately reassured. A jocose remark of the Captain's at dinner next day that he supposed " our old friend, Jeffery, had got housed by this time," was enough to satisfy Spencer that there were in fact houses in Sombrero and that the Captain thought so too. So the Master said, but with a skipper like Lake *quieta non movere* was probably a well-understood maxim in the ship.

The *Recruit* continued cruising for some weeks before she touched at Barbadoes, and on the affair being reported to Admiral Sir Alexander Cochrane, the Commander-in-Chief on the station, he promptly ordered the ship back to Sombrero. She did not arrive there, however, until the 11th February, 1808, nearly two months after Jeffery had been marooned, and the landing party found no trace of him. Part of a pair of trousers that could not be identified as his was picked up, but the examination of the island was made in a cursory fashion, as if it were—as no doubt it was—more or less a matter of form. They had a good day or two's shooting, and established beyond doubt that Sombrero was an uninhabited island. Captain Lake is said to have made the common *ex post facto* exclamation that he would have given a large sum rather than have the business happen. The Admiral took a curiously lenient view, best shown by quoting his own words, written nearly two years later. " I was well aware," he said, " of the irregularity of the proceeding at the time it occurred, and when it was reported to me I immediately sent Captain Lake back to the island to take the man off, but he was gone : and having heard soon after of the circumstances being reported in an American paper and of the man's arrival there, which assured me of his safety, I consented after seriously admonishing Captain Lake to let the business rest." No further steps were taken at this time to ascertain what had really happened to Jeffery, and in the comfortable assurance of a report in an American newspaper the matter did rest until well into the following year. Then, more or less by accident, the news of this " irregular proceeding " got to England.

There was in the West Indies a man named Charles Morgan Thomas, who had been a purser in the Navy but had resigned his warrant to Sir A. Cochrane. He wanted to return to England, and he averred that Cochrane detained him on the station against his will on suspicion of having been fraudulent in some matter of stores. There is no need to inquire into the grounds of Thomas's personal grievances. The Admiral's methods were occasionally high-handed—if we are to believe the American skipper quoted by Mr. Roosevelt, in his account of the War of 1812 : on the other hand, there was a good deal of Mr. Pecksniff about ex-purser Morgan Thomas. On the 24th March, 1809, he wrote from the *Neptune,* at Martinique, to the Right Hon. Charles Bathurst, the Member for Bristol, to which place he belonged,

complaining of the difficulties put in his way by
Cochrane : and then as a sort of make-weight he
added, " I deem it a duty I owe to humanity to
inform you that Captain Lake when commander
of the *Recruit*, set a man belonging to that vessel
on shore at Sombrero, an uninhabited island in
the Atlantic Archipelago, where he died thro'
hunger or otherwise, for more was never heard of
him.   This was likewise known to Sir A. Cochrane,
who suffered this titled murderer to escape, and
he now has command of the *Ulysses*."   Early
in 1809 Lake had in fact been given another
command.   Bathurst wrote to the Lords of the
Admiralty, enclosing this letter, and it became
necessary to take the matter up.   In July, we
find Lake replying to Mr. Secretary Pole, and
whilst admitting that the man had been landed,
blandly repeating Cochrane's hearsay about Jeffery
having been taken off by an American vessel,
and concluding by making reflections on the
character of Thomas.   Mr. Secretary Pole then
took a legal opinion, and was told that Lake was
liable both criminally and civilly to the party
injured, as well as to a court-martial under the
Regulations.   Cochrane was communicated with
in November and wrote from Halifax harbour
the letter already quoted ; still deprecating the
idea of a court-martial, and winding up by stating
that Sombrero was close to Anguilla, and that
vessels were constantly passing.   In December,
three Navy captains sat at Portsmouth to in-
vestigate the affair and made a report.   It was
not until the 5th February, 1810, that Lake was
put upon his trial in that port before a court-

martial sitting on board the *Gladiator*, which
decided, notwithstanding the prisoner's admission
in writing that he had put the man ashore, to
hear the evidence. Spencer and half a dozen
more of the *Recruit's* people deposed to the facts
of the landing as outlined above. Captain Lake's
defence, prepared for him and read by a barrister,
was merely a lengthy palliation. His two points
were that he thought the island was inhabited
and that Admiral Cochrane had let him off with
a reprimand. He was sentenced to be dismissed
from His Majesty's Service.

Beyond the alleged report in an unnamed
American newspaper nothing was yet known of
the fate of Jeffery. Thomas's letter was printed
in the *Times* of the 8th March, with a demand
for further inquiry. On the 3rd April, there was
an animated debate on the matter in the House
of Commons, with Sir Francis Burdett as the
champion of the oppressed. He adopted the
phrase used by Thomas and denounced Lake's
act as murder. More moderate people pointed
out that as nobody yet knew the man was dead
no Grand Jury would find a true bill even for
manslaughter. Two Service members, whilst
guarding themselves against being taken to ap-
prove the deed, testified, as in duty bound, the
one to the abundance of eggs upon Sombrero,
the other to the impossibility of anyone being
obliged to remain there more than twenty-four
hours if he waved his hat. Mr. Whitbread moved
an address to His Majesty that directions might
be given for a search in all settlements abroad,
in the Navy, and also in foreign countries as far

as possible, to ascertain whether Jeffery was still alive. This was agreed to unanimously, and the resolution of the House was circulated by the Admiralty with a description of Jeffery appended.

The replies which were gathered from various quarters displayed the small discrepancies which were to be expected, but they agreed that Jeffery had been rescued by an American vessel. Ultimately, the testimony of the American skipper who had actually effected the rescue, taken at Corunna and duly authenticated, set all doubt at rest. Captain John Adams, master of the schooner *Adams*, of Marblehead, Mass., deposed that he had taken the lad off after a stay of eight days in Sombrero " extremely reduced and exhausted," but that he recovered, and had gone to Beverly, near Marblehead, to work at his old trade of blacksmith. Inquiries made at Polperro in Cornwall, where Jeffery's mother lived, showed that rumours of the rescue had already reached there, and were being circulated with sensational details about the castaway having been constrained to gnaw his own flesh. Some capital was made out of the fact that he had not himself written to his mother by the usual people who, having made sure of a tragic *dénouement*, were reluctant to be baulked of it. It appears by the doggerel afterwards circulated about him—it may be read in *Naval Songs and Ballads*—that he was an only son ; but nothing we know of the youth's character suggests excess of piety. It is possible that Jeffery after his experiences ignorantly thought it safer to be temporarily undutiful than to run any risks with the long arm of the British Admiralty. His fears, if he had any, were presently allayed, and on the 22nd October, 1810, he arrived in London. The Admiralty gave him a free discharge from the Service, and the friends of Captain Lake got up a subscription for him. According to his own statement, as reported in the *Gentleman's Magazine*, he subsisted during his week on the island solely upon the rain water in the crevices of the rocks, and was in the last stage of starvation when Captain Adams found him. There is quite a modern touch in the further remark that " several persons were desirous of engaging him to exhibit himself." With this proposal, however, Jeffery could not comply. It was obviously inexpedient that he should remain in evidence longer than necessary, and it appears that he obtained his discharge from the Service only on condition that he immediately quitted the metropolitan focus. So the " Governor of Sombrero," as the people at Marblehead had dubbed him, went down to Cornwall to see his mother " in high spirits " and as far as I know appeared in public no more.

The busybody Morgan Thomas, who had wanted to slip out of the Navy in the West Indies, was now writing to Mr. Whitbread to complain that he had been dismissed from it for playing the informer : and after asserting the disinterested character and philanthropy of the motives which led him originally to address Mr. Bathurst, the member for Bristol, he offered to continue in the rôle. " I cannot conclude, sir," he wrote, " without acquainting you that I have abundant information which, bad as the times are, will still furnish matter of astonishment." What his further revelations were, or whether he made any, does not appear. Justice sometimes employs the strangest instruments.

Captain Lake had been in trouble in 1809 for endangering discipline and for drunkenness whilst in the *Ulysses*, and though a court-martial had acquitted him it remarked a want of correctness on his part as to the first charge and recommended him to be in future more circumspect in his conduct as to the second. The witnesses in the Jeffery inquiry describe him as " passionate " ; and he was perhaps to be as much commiserated as his victim for being fairly conspicuously unsuited to his situation. The statement of an ex-marine of the *Recruit* that Lake kept him gagged with an iron hammer in his mouth from five in the evening till noon next day for expressing pity for Jeffery must be received with caution. It was made after Lake's downfall. But still, considerable originality in making the punishment fit the supposed crime is to be discerned in the records of the period. The planting of a duly labelled thief on an uninhabited island has something of the same irony, whether it occurred to Captain Lake or not ; and another captain admitted on being tried for oppression about the same time that he compelled drunkards to drink a quart of salt water before he flogged them as the best and quickest way of bringing them to recognise the folly of their proclivity. One hardly wonders that desertion to the Americans was rife at this time.

VII

THE CRUISE OF THE "PYLADES"

ALL the biographers of Lord Stowell, the famous Judge of the Admiralty Court during the Napoleonic wars, have alluded to the trial before him of the young Marquis of Sligo in the year 1812, because it led to what the latest of them, Mr. Roscoe, calls "the one mistake of his life"—his second marriage. Naturally they have not done more than give the barest outline of the facts which resulted in the appearance of the Marquis at the Admiralty Sessions at the Old Bailey, since Sir William Scott, as he then still was, only comes into the story as the too paternal admonisher of a youthful misdemeanant whose distressed mother he made his wife within four months of passing sentence on her son. In like manner the lapse from perfect wisdom which created so much amusement at the time amongst "the wicked wags of the town," and brought some years of discomfort to the sexagenarian judge, lies outside, or at least at the very end of, our narrative. But the doings of the Marquis in the Mediterranean two years earlier, upon which was founded a charge of inducing seamen to desert from His Majesty's Fleet, and of concealing them on board his own yacht, are not—at this time of day—without their humorous aspect, and they have some bearing also upon naval life in the first years of the nineteenth century. It is proposed, therefore, briefly to review the evidence which was given at this curious trial.

The case is noteworthy, moreover, as being apparently without precedent. The law officers of the Crown, Sir Vicary Gibbs and Sir Thomas Plumer, when consulted by the Admiralty in 1811, gave a guarded opinion. They were not aware, they said, that any specific punishment was inflicted on persons not belonging to the Fleet for enticing mariners to desert from His Majesty's Service, but as persons in the Service might be court-martialled for the offence under the Articles of War of 1749, contained in the statute of George the Second of that year, they conceived it to be a misdemeanour in anybody else, and they advised that Lord Sligo should be put upon his trial. Seeing that desertion from the Navy was not an uncommon offence then and aforetime, it is curious that there should have been no recorded instances of the bringing to book of aiders and abbettors ; and it was perhaps due to the attitude of contrition displayed at and before his trial by the defendant in this particular case that no technical point of law traversing the opinion of the law officers was raised on his behalf. But penitent though the prisoner showed himself, there was a certain rigour in the conduct of the prosecution. No doubt it was war-time ; and, moreover, it came out in evidence that the Fleet in the Mediterranean was in 1810 nearly two thousand men short of its proper complement. The indictment alleged that the Marquis was responsible for the carrying off of some seventeen seamen—though the

Admiralty was unable to supply the names of more than about half of them—" to the weakening of the naval forces of His Majesty, His Dominions and subjects." This was a serious charge enough, but there were others included in the indictment. There was also a count for assault and false imprisonment of certain of his captives—a charge which broke down entirely ; and as if this were not enough, allegations were made at the trial of the defendant's inhumanity in setting them free in outlandish places when he found he was burning his fingers with them. It is, of course, frequently very difficult to do right when once you have done wrong.

Let us now endeavour to piece together the story of these misdoings. In the spring of 1810 the second Marquis of Sligo, a grandson and namesake of Admiral Earl Howe, was just twenty-two years of age, and had recently succeeded to the title and the family estates. He arrived in the Mediterranean with a letter of introduction from Admiral George Martin to Captain Spranger of H.M.S. *Warrior*, then the senior naval officer at Malta. "Freshly imbued with the associations of a classical education," as one of his apologists has naïvely put it, he desired to cruise amongst the Greek Islands. His college friend, Lord Byron, was already in those waters : in Byron's recently published " Correspondence " there occur several references to the *Pylades* and its owner : nothing could possibly have been more natural and even praiseworthy in a man of Lord Sligo's position than these beginnings. Accordingly, a brig named the *Pylades* was hired for the use

of the young nobleman : she had formerly belonged
to the Austrian Navy, and carried sixteen guns.
She was now fitted out not merely as a pleasure
yacht, but furnished also with letters of marque.
It is probable that this privateering equipment,
and the consequential desire of Lord Sligo to
have the most efficient men he could get behind
those sixteen guns, first prompted the proceedings that led to his appearance in the dock at the
Old Bailey.

Captain Spranger was extremely kind to his
lordship's nautical aspirations. He lent him
riggers and carpenters and gunners, all of them
part of the *Warrior's* crew, to assist in fitting out
the *Pylades*. The Marquis, on his part, greatly
admired the four picked seamen of the *Warrior's*
gig, in which during these operations he seems
to have been frequently passing to and fro between
the two vessels. He had observed to the Captain
what remarkably fine, " clever-looking " men they
were. Not long afterwards two of them, named
Lloyd and Lee, were missing from the *Warrior*.
The Captain could not understand it. As he
himself said, the gig's crew were very trusty
seamen, who had never been absent or irregular,
and though frequently suffered to go ashore
without a midshipman, had never abused that
confidence during the three years they had
been told off for that boat. He thought the
men's desertion the more remarkable because
there were three years' wages due to them
at the time. One sees what he meant, but
there might perhaps be another way of looking
at it.

F

The *Warrior* was on the point of leaving Malta, and a talk with his officers resulted in Captain Spranger going on board the *Pylades* to interview the Marquis. The young man affected to be much hurt by the suspicions of the *Warrior's* people. Did Spranger think him so ungracious as to steal the *Warrior's* men after all the civilities he had received ? He owned that some of the men lent to him for fitting-out had indeed offered to desert, but he, the Marquis had refused to accept them. Confronted with this attitude, the Captain felt constrained to content himself with requesting that should the missing seamen come to the *Pylades* they should be given up to the commanding officer at Malta. The Marquis promised, and Spranger sent him a description of them when he got back to his ship. He had not caused the *Pylades'* crew to be mustered for his inspection. The seamen he saw appeared to be foreigners, in number between twenty and thirty, though he knew that the Marquis, going a-privateering, had talked of taking fifty men with him. But Spranger's polite omission to search the brig did not matter, because, whether with or without Lord Sligo's knowledge, Messrs. Lloyd and Lee were at that moment secreted ashore in a house tenanted by the Marquis. It should be added that a man named Nedin, who was employed by the Marquis to obtain seamen, and who had found these sailors their quarters in that house, denied on oath that his master had any knowledge of their being there. And, even according to the evidence of Captain Spranger himself, men were constantly deserting on their own account—

hardly a matter for wonder if their pay was three
years in arrear.

The *Warrior* left Malta early on May 13th.
On that day William Elden, gunner's mate of the
Montagu, another 74 in the harbour, and five or
six other seamen belonging to the same ship were
on shore on leave. According to the story afterwards told by them, they were met by the mate
of the *Pylades* and two of Lord Sligo's servants in
livery, invited into a wine shop and plied with
liquor. They said they remembered nothing more
until they found themselves next morning in the
pump-well or cable-tier of his lordship's brig,
which was then under way. Richard Cooke,
bosun's mate of the *Montagu*, said that hearing
that his shipmates were in the *Pylades* he went
aboard her to make sure of them, and that the
defendant, when he found out who he was, ordered
the waterman's boat away and himself below.
If the jury had believed this, they could hardly
have acquitted Lord Sligo of false imprisonment ;
but Cooke's evidence must be read in the light of
the fact that he had been heard to vow to do his
worst in revenge for being left ashore at Patmos
afterwards. Late in the evening of May 13th,
or early next day, the *Pylades* sailed, having on
board the two seamen from the *Warrior*, ten from
the *Montagu*, two each from the *Hind* frigate and
the *Black Joke* lugger, and one from the *Shearwater*
brig.

From Malta the yacht went to Palermo, and
thence to Messina. Not much weight need be
given to the statements made by the men as to
the measures taken to prevent them leaving the

ship at these places—the posting of Italians as
sentries at the gangways and so forth. They are
only relevant to the charge of false imprisonment,
which fell to the ground completely, and they
are inconsistent with William Elden's evidence,
that he was given leave to go ashore at Palermo
and returned to the brig without surrendering to
any King's ship, although there were two British
74's in that port at the time. It is to be remembered that the men's account of what happened
to them was first given when some of them were
on their trial for desertion before a court-martial.
They had to put the best face they could on their
disappearance, and having alleged duress and
imprisonment in the *Pylades*, they could hardly
do otherwise than stick to their first statements
up to the time when they came to be examined
at the Old Bailey. It is more likely that the
bounties which the Marquis had openly offered
for English sailors—not men-of-war's men, of
course, though there would be more such men at
Malta than English merchant seamen—and the
advance of twenty dollars apiece for a month's
wages, which was in fact paid to the men at
Palermo, were more effectual in retaining them
than any number of Italian sentries would have
been : and if it is true, as was stated, that the
brig was searched for deserters at Palermo by
an officer from H.M.S. *Cumberland*, it is difficult
to suppose that seventeen able-bodied men who
were themselves sincerely desirous to surrender
could have been concealed from him. The
solitary sailor belonging to the *Shearwater* did
leave the yacht at Messina ; but Lord Sligo

stated that so far from it being an "escape" he himself dismissed the man. On the other hand, the sailing master of the *Pylades*, one Llewellyn, had admitted on cross-examination in his evidence before the court-martial that the prisoners, Elden and the rest, had all along said they were sorry they were on board. Very likely they were, with the probability of a court-martial with power to order a flogging looming ahead of them; but herein was another motive to stay where they were and await events.

As time went on and the men remained on board they doubtless felt that their case grew worse. Lord Sligo endeavoured to reassure them by means which it must be admitted were more ingenious than straightforward. He knew that the men's names would probably be forwarded from their own ships to the commanders of cruisers, and he invented fictitious names in which he entered them on the books of his own ship. His "slimness" even went a little bit further. At Messina he obtained from Admiral Martin a protection against impressment covering forty men, of course on the understanding that he had no deserters on board. These protections were occasionally granted by Admirals on foreign stations, and seem to have been issued in blank for a specific number of men, whose names and descriptions were filled in afterwards as they were engaged. This seems to have been done here with the aliases invented for the occasion. Elden, the gunner's mate from the *Montagu*, deposed that he heard the Marquis tell the ship's company that they had now nothing to fear unless their old ships fell in with them, and they were recognised by their old shipmates. It is impossible to doubt that Lord Sligo was well aware he had Navy men on board long before he got to Messina ; indeed, he afterwards admitted that he suspected it on the evening of the departure from Malta. The fine fellows of the *Warrior's* gig he had known by sight for weeks, and both Elden and a seaman named Storey swore they told him they belonged to the *Montagu* the first day out. What happened when H.M.S. *Active* fell in with the *Pylades* off the coast of Calabria was therefore incapable of any defence that a court of law could accept. On May 30th that sloop-of-war, on the look-out for deserters, chased the brig and fired several shots at her before bringing her to. Meanwhile, the men-of-war's men on board the yacht were bundled into the after-hold under the cabin floor, the hatch closed upon them, and potato sacks placed on the top of it. They said again that they only underwent this indignity under compulsion, but when they made the statement these misguided mariners were very much between the devil and the deep sea. Lieutenant Hayes of the *Active* came aboard and mustered the *Pylades'* crew by the watch-list. He had a list of the men wanted from the *Warrior* and the *Montagu*, but, strangely enough, he could not find their names set down anywhere in the list given to him by the Marquis, nor did he see anybody at all like a man-of-war's man amongst the seamen, chiefly foreigners, who were paraded before him by that gentleman. The two midshipmen who searched below found only a sick

Italian in a hammock. Lord Sligo, who is said
by one witness to have assisted the officers by
holding a candle, told the Lieutenant that the
men he was seeking for probably left the *Pylades*
at Messina. Afterwards he excused this *suggestio
falsi* upon the ground of humanity towards these
unfortunate tars ; and, indeed, it is evident that
he by now felt himself to blame for whatever
might happen to them. In the letter of apology
which he sent to Captain Spranger from Con-
stantinople in November, he declared in effect
that the thought present to his mind when he
concealed the men was " At worst I shall only
have to pay a fine, whilst if I give these fellows
up they will all be flogged."

It is equally clear that though he succeeded
in baffling the *Active*, he must by this time have
wished the men out of his yacht. After touching
at Milo the *Pylades* went to Patmos, and there
Elden and other seamen—not all of them deserters
from men-of-war—went ashore. They alleged
that they were left there on purpose ; on the
other hand, the witnesses for the Marquis declared
that the Blue Peter was hoisted and guns fired to
recall them before the ship sailed, and that even
then she stood off and on near the land during
the night. As a matter of fact they were left
behind, and making their way to Scio attempted
to rejoin the ship at that place. They came off
to the *Pylades* in a boat, but Lord Sligo refused
to allow the greater part of them on board, though
he caused their belongings to be restored to them.
Ultimately they were sent by the British Consul
to Smyrna. In February, 1811, they were tried

for desertion by a court-martial at Port Mahon and found guilty. But Elden had eighteen years' service in the Navy to his credit : he had been in the *Montagu* six of them. Captain Mowbray said of him and a seaman named Fisher that there was no trust compatible with their situation he would not have reposed in them, and of the rest that he had never met with better men in the course of his service. The sentence of flogging which was passed upon them was not carried out.

Later in the year, as already mentioned, the matter was laid before the law officers to advise, and an indictment was preferred against the Marquis at the Admiralty Sessions in February, 1812. To this in June he formally pleaded not guilty, and gave sureties for his appearance at the trial, which came on in December before the Judge of the Admiralty Court, and Lord Ellenborough and Mr. Baron Thompson, the Common Law Judges associated with him in the Commission. The case naturally occasioned some stir. The Duke of Clarence had a seat on the Bench, though the story of the defendant's mother, the Dowager Marchioness of Sligo, being present in court and sending a grateful note up to the presiding judge, her future husband, must be regarded as a romantic invention. The hearing lasted from the forenoon of the 16th until (such was the judicial fashion of those days) 2 a.m. the next morning. The prisoner through his counsel would now have pleaded guilty to all the counts save those charging him with assault and imprisonment, but Lord Ellenborough ruled that he must plead guilty or not guilty to the whole indictment, and the whole story was investigated. Such defence as could be made was to the effect that if men-of-war's men had been brought on board the *Pylades*, it had been done by defendant's servants against his orders and without his knowledge. But the subsequent concealment of the men from the officers of the *Active* was not disputed, nor indeed could it be after the apologetic letters which the Marquis had written, first to Captain Spranger, and afterwards to the Admiralty admitting and attempting to justify it on the score of his concern for the men themselves. In the event Lord Sligo was found guilty on all the counts except that of assault and false imprisonment. If the evidence of the " enticing " seems, as far as one can tell from the bare records of the trial, to have been not particularly strong, the " harbouring," however excellent its belated motive, had certainly taken place. The defendant was sentenced next day to pay a fine of £5000 and to be imprisoned in Newgate for four months. An exculpatory affidavit by the prisoner expressing his contrition was allowed to be read by his counsel after verdict given. It probably had no effect upon the sentence, but it may have influenced the moving homily as to defendant's duty to his country which (with such unfortunate results for himself) Sir William Scott delivered in passing it. It was no doubt desirable that an example should be made ; but at least it may be said that this youth of twenty-two was not long in recognising the foolishness of his prank, and that the Navy got the best of its " clever-looking " seamen back again.

VIII

THE trial of the ten foreign sailors who, on the 24th July, 1845, stood in the dock at the Devon Assizes charged with wilful murder, is commonly found in contemporary journals under the heading of " The Spanish Pirates," though, in fact, they were not Spaniards; as to the other word it is one which has always been useful when unprecedented, or at least unanticipated, violence has taken place upon the high seas. It is true that there had been signed, as far back as 1826, a Convention between Great Britain and Brazil, to which country the men belonged, by which it was declared that it should not be lawful for subjects of the Emperor of Brazil to engage in the slave trade, the carrying of which, it was added, should thereafter be deemed to be piracy; but Brazil had nevertheless made no alteration in her municipal laws upon the subject, and up to 1845 no Brazilian was liable to any penalty in the courts of Brazil for engaging in it. A contemporary newspaper commenting upon the prisoners' complexions, which were indubitably swarthy, founded its opinion that they appeared well fitted for the trade of pirate entirely upon that circumstance; but, in fact, when it came to formulating the charge against them, Francisco de Santo Serva, Janus

Majavel, and the other tawny seamen were not charged with piracy. They were indicted for murder : and though they had undoubtedly slain a number of British sailors it became in the circumstances a very grave question whether it was within the power of an English court to convict them even of that. The consideration of that question on three separate occasions well illustrates the painstaking character of the administration of English justice : but the story is also worthy of being retold because it shows that the rules of international law, nebulous as they sometimes seem, may yet be a determining factor in the decision of a purely national court. The trial is also noteworthy because after the points of law involved had been argued before the full Bench of Common Law Judges, their Lordships desired to have further light thereon, and the case was again discussed before them by Doctors of the Civil Law from Doctors' Commons, which was still the home of the expert in international legal problems. This was the last occasion, I think, upon which the assistance of the civilians was sought by Westminster Hall.

The chain of events that led to the trial of these ten foreigners at Exeter is at first sight rather a complicated one, but it is not incapable of being straightened out. The *Felicidade*, a Brazilian schooner, undoubtedly fitted out for the reception of slaves, was captured by the boats of H.M.S. *Wasp* on the 22nd February, 1845. She had, however, no slaves on board at the time, as she was on her voyage from the Brazils to Africa, but it was patent that she

was going there in order to obtain a cargo of
them; the log of the *Wasp* is careful to state
that in her hold were stores of water, and beans,
and rice, as well as plates and pots for a large
number of slaves, and when stopped she was
within sixteen miles of the African coast. No
resistance was made by the *Felicidade's* captain,
a Brazilian named Cerquiera; the greater part
of her crew were at once conveyed on board the
Wasp, and Lieutenant Stupart, who had been
in charge of the boats, took command of the
schooner, having with him Mr. Palmer, a midshipman, and sixteen seamen belonging to the
man-of-war, as a prize crew. The legality of
this capture would in any case have been doubtful
for reasons that will be explained presently, but
it became a crucial point in consequence of what
happened during the next few days. The captain
of the *Wasp* instead of sending the *Felicidade*
into Sierra Leone for the legality of her capture
to be investigated before a court established
there for such inquiries, kept her in company
with his own ship until the 27th February : and
on that day, observing a suspicious vessel in the
distance, he signalled to Stupart to give chase.
The details of that pursuit need not detain us :
it was a stern chase and a long one, but it may be
pointed out that it was a mistake on the part of
the *Wasp* to employ as the instrument of a fresh
detention a vessel which had not been adjudicated
her prize. The *Felicidade* ultimately overhauled
the stranger, which proved to be the Brazilian
brigantine *Echo*, commanded by Francisco de
Santo Serva (who gives his name to the Assize

case), and which had on board a crew of 26 men and a cargo of over four hundred slaves. She also surrendered to Lieutenant Stupart without resistance : but it is obvious that with only Mr. Palmer and sixteen men under his command that officer was in considerable difficulty in assuring to himself undisputed possession of the two vessels. It is to be remembered that the *Wasp* had been left far behind, two days having been spent before the suspicious brigantine could be come up with. The captain of the captured *Echo*, and his crew of twenty-six, together with Captain Cerquiera and Majavel, the cook of the *Felicidade*, who were still in that ship, made a total of twenty-nine Brazilians to be looked after. In addition, the condition of the four hundred negroes in the *Echo* was such as demanded the English lieutenant's charitable attention. Lieutenant Stupart tried more than one distribution of his forces between the schooner and the brigantine, and the fact shows some uneasiness on his part. Finally, on the morning after the capture of the *Echo*, there were left on board the *Felicidade* only Mr. Palmer, the midshipman (in command), and nine British seamen to cope with thirteen Brazilians. Within an hour of parting company with the *Echo*, ten of these, led by Serva and Majavel, killed or threw overboard Palmer and the rest of the British. Captain Cerquiera, and two negroes who originally had been part of the *Echo's* crew, were dissenting parties to the affray, and the success of the rising against their captors by the other ten seems, if the evidence of Cerquiera given at their trial is to be believed, to have been considerably aided by the carelessness of the victims. He said that just before the attack, three of the British seamen were asleep, including the one posted as sentry at the hatchway whence the Brazilians issued. Mr. Palmer appears to have just had a bath and was standing aft wiping himself and conversing with the quartermaster. That any attempt to re-take the ship would be made evidently never occurred to this happy-go-lucky midshipman, or the knives of the Brazilian sailors would hardly have been left in their belts. It was an affair of cold steel.

Having swept the *Felicidade's* deck of the English, Serva seems to have had some idea of re-taking the *Echo*. He hoisted the Brazilian flag, hailed the other vessel and informed her what he had accomplished : but his warlike operations were confined to loading a gun and firing a shot or two at her. The *Felicidade* then bore away ; probably it was useless for the *Echo* to chase, as the *Felicidade* had but just shown that she was the better sailer of the two. Three days later, however, on the 6th March, she was met by another British cruiser, H.M.S. *Star*, which again detained and searched her. The suspicion of the *Star's* officers was naturally aroused by what they found on board. The wounds upon the bodies of most of the *Felicidade's* crew could not be satisfactorily explained, nor the marks of blood upon the deck : and there was also found in the ship a copy of Herschel's *Astronomy* with Lieutenant Stupart's name in it. In the end Cerquiera and the two blacks revealed what had occurred and the rest of the crew were put in irons, ultimately to be sent to England for trial. The prisoners and the three witnesses against them having been taken out of the *Felicidade*, Lieutenant Wilson of the *Star* was then put in charge, with orders to take her into Sierra Leone. She was, however, capsized by a squall before getting there, Wilson and his men barely escaping with their lives on a raft, which was picked up at sea after many days by H.M.S. *Cygnet :* and thus she was never condemned as a prize by the Sierra Leone Mixed Tribunal. Her fate after her second capture by the *Star* is not material to our present story : but the log of that man-of-war, recording the stopping and boarding of her, states that twenty-one prisoners were taken out of her. If so, the unfortunate Palmer and his crew had been left outnumbered by two to one.

An English criminal court had to decide what was the status of the *Felicidade* by international law at the time when her deck was being sprinkled with the blood of Mr. Midshipman Palmer and the nine bluejackets from the *Wasp*. The rule in general is that every ship on the high seas is, as it were, part of the territory of the State whose flag she flies ; inviolable, unless some treaty for a specific purpose gives the men-of-war of another nation a right, always to be punctilously exercised, of interference. Had it been so exercised here ? The *Felicidade* was a foreign ship : had what happened before the affray so changed her character that an English court of justice had jurisdiction over acts done in her ?

It might have been doubted beforehand whether an Assize Court afforded the best possible tribunal to determine such a question and the sequel of the trial in the country was to deepen any such doubt. Not that " the Spanish Pirates " were not treated with perfect fairness. They had the benefit of a jury *de medietate linguæ*, composed half of Englishmen and half of foreigners, which the tenderness of the law of England had from very early times interposed between an accused alien and national prejudice. They were defended with great skill and learning : some of them by Serjeant Manning, a leader on the Western Circuit, the others by Mr. Robert Collier, a young barrister who became in later life Lord Monkswell, the Judge, and whose brilliant efforts in this case are said to have first established his professional reputation. But Mr. Baron Platt waved aside the points of law raised by these gentlemen on behalf of their clients : the killing of Palmer and the others was abundantly proved and the judge refused to reserve what he probably deemed to be mere technicalities for the consideration of the full Court of Queen's Bench. The jury found seven of the ten prisoners guilty and they were sentenced to death.

Yet the points taken on their behalf were not wholly technicalities. If the capture of these two vessels from the Brazilians had been illegal and wrong might they not be justified in resisting it, even at a subsequent time, should the opportunity occur, as they certainly would have been justified in resisting an initial interference with them, if unwarranted ? The capture of the *Felici-*

dade, it was contended, was illegal because she had no slaves on board; undoubtedly there had been incorporated in the Convention of 1826, already mentioned, an instruction to the effect that ships on board of which no slaves were found, but intended for the purposes of the traffic, should not be detained on any pretence whatever. There was warrant for stopping and searching the *Felicidade*, but none for keeping her. The capture of the *Echo* was irregular in that the vessel stopping her was not a ship of Her Majesty's Navy, but only the *Felicidade*, illegally detained in the possession of the British. It was to be remembered on his behalf that Serva, the prisoner chiefly concerned in instigating the attack on Palmer and the English prize-crew, had been the *Echo's* captain. On the other hand, the view taken by the prosecution and adopted by Mr. Baron Platt, was that the *Felicidade*, whilst detained for the purpose of submitting the circumstances to the judgment of the Court at Sierra Leone, was lawfully in the possession of the British and her deck as much within the jurisdiction of Her Majesty as the deck of H.M.S. *Wasp*. But meanwhile the captain of the *Wasp* had been using her as a sort of fast tender to assist his ship in her further operations.

There was considerable doubt in the minds of many people whether in these circumstances, and having regard to the grave questions of international law involved, the Judge of Assize was right in his refusal to allow them further to be considered. A representation was made by the Brazilian Minister to the Secretary of State

G

for Foreign Affairs: pressure seems to have been brought to bear on Mr. Baron Platt, and on the 4th August, only four days before the date fixed for the execution of the condemned, it was announced in both Houses of Parliament that he had determined to reserve the points raised. The prisoners were then respited, pending the decision of the full Bench of Judges.

The case came on for hearing before a Court composed of thirteen of Her Majesty's Judges on the 15th of November following (the Court for Crown Cases Reserved was not established until some three years later), when the same Counsel appeared for the defence who had conducted it at the Assizes. It would be out of place to attempt here even a summary of their argument: some of the points to the establishment of which it was directed have already been briefly indicated. But after hearing these gentlemen and the reply of Mr. Godson for the Crown, the Judges were still unprepared to give a decision: and accordingly on the 3rd December the case was argued again before twelve of the same thirteen by civilians practising in the Admiralty Court, which at that time and for some dozen years afterwards was a close preserve of the doctors of the civil law at Doctors' Commons. The scene on this occasion was the Hall of Serjeants' Inn, and Dr. Addams and Dr. Hardy took the places of Manning and Collier, whilst Sir John Dodson, the Advocate General, and Dr. Phillimore, the Admiralty Advocate (offices now long defunct), represented the Crown. Afterwards a large majority of the Judges held that the conviction

for murder could not be upheld : the two dissen-
tients being Lord Chief Justice Denman and,
not unnaturally, Mr. Baron Platt, who had tried
the case at Exeter. Serva and the others were
therefore sent back to Brazil at the expense of
the British Government.

Thereupon the *Times*, begging the question in
a rather angry leader which quoted Coke's description of a pirate as an enemy of the human race
by the law of nations, went on to say that " acting
on this universal law " British cruisers had captured many Brazilian slavers, and that it was to
be hoped that being now further fortified by a
new Act of Parliament they would not be fright-
ened by the fate of the unfortunate officer of the
Wasp, or the decision of the fifteen Judges of
England, but would continue their exertions
" in a high and honourable cause." The Slave
Trade (Brazils) Act had received the Royal
assent between the date of the trial at Exeter
and the arguments in London. In fact, by a
coincidence, the debate on the Bill in the Commons
had taken place on the 24th July, the day on
which Mr. Baron Platt was trying the prisoners
in the country. The Bill was described by its
chief opponent in the House, Mr. Thomas Milner-
Gibson, as a penal act against a friendly power
and its object as an attempt, if the Brazilians
would not abolish the slave trade themselves, to
abolish it for them. Mr. Milner-Gibson was a
yachtsman well versed in nautical affairs : it is
said that he was the last person to cruise in the
Mediterranean with a free pass from the Dey of
Algiers—though that interesting fact need not

lead us to suppose him in any way sympathetic towards " pirates." But he probably understood better than members who had never navigated ships of their own, the anarchy that must result from unwarrantable interferences with a foreign flag upon the high seas. We may perhaps regard this Act of Parliament as another illustration of the lengths to which a consciousness of " a high and honourable cause " may lead those who are proud of it. As to the unfortunate affair which led to all this commotion—the seizure of the *Felicidade*—its legal aspect could not of course be affected by legislation passed after the event. The Brazilian Government, as a long protest filling three columns of the *Times* newspaper shows, continued to characterise it as " an infringement of the sovereignty and independence of Brazil." Not very different at bottom was the view taken by the great majority of the Judges : and the value of the judiciary as a corrective alike to popular sentiment and an over-zealous executive was once more vindicated.

IX

AN ACT OF STATE

DURING the first half of the nineteenth century England had made the abolition of the slave trade " her own cause." It was with a newly awakened conscience that she did so, for the traffic had only been declared illegal for her subjects in 1807. But her conscience was in advance of that of many other States, and the zeal of the newly converted is proverbial ; as a consequence there were, as we have seen, lapses in her regard for the chapter-and-verse view of international justice. Energetic naval officers, when instructed to do all in their power to inter-fere either with the trade of an enemy in time of war, or a particular traffic like the slave trade in time of peace, are not always restrained from doing things that seem helpful by dicta in the books of jurists that such things are not done. The discussion of principles comes afterwards ; and probably no more amusing instance of such a belated discussion has been recorded than is afforded by that which centred round the actions for trespass brought against Captain the Honour-able Joseph Denman, R.N., in the English Court of Exchequer by Señors Tomas Buron, Angel Jimenez, and Pedro Martinez—actions which arose out of Great Britain's determination to suppress the slave trade. The antecedent facts at any rate have a humour of their own.

In the year 1840 the islands at the mouth of the Gallinas River on the West Coast of Africa were a well-known centre for the collection of unhappy negroes in readiness for shipping them across the Atlantic. There were eight barracoons, or factories, at Dombocorro and other places a little higher up the stream. They contained large quantities of cotton and woollen goods, gunpowder and spirituous liquors for the purposes of the traffic with the hinterland; and some of them were defended by guns in case the negotiations of the traders with the native potentates should take an untoward turn. One of these factories was (at the present day quite inexplicably) known as " Paisley " : the others had Spanish or native names. It is stated that the annual number of slaves exported from Gallinas about this time amounted to eighteen thousand.

Watching the mouth of the river from outside was a part of Her Britannic Majesty's Navy. Its business there was described, just a little loosely, even in official documents, as a " blockade," but it had, of course, no right to interfere with shipping properly using the river either going in or coming out, except in the case where a slaver might try to give it the slip. This, however, was naturally enough to earn for it the active hostility of the Spaniards owning the factories ashore ; and this rancour had gone so far that on one occasion when a boat belonging to the English men-of-war got into difficulties, the slave merchants prevented the native longshoremen giving the boat's crew the assistance the negroes were about to render.

There was, however, a third party to what was about to take place. Such rights of sovereignty as existed at the mouth of the Gallinas River in 1840 were vested in an elderly king called Siacca. They were not particularly obvious, if it were true, as this retiring old gentleman afterwards stated, that the islands on his sea-front had been occupied in despite of him by the Spanish traders ; but it became in the sequel highly desirable to resuscitate them, to the extent of recognising his kingly right to contract a valid treaty with the British Government through Captain Denman, its representative.

Not the least curious feature of the story is the fact that it begins with an incident wholly unconnected with the slave trade. King Siacca had a son named Manna, who at Dombocorro was no doubt a prince, and as surely a little high-handed in the conduct of his private business. A woman of colour, named Nelson, a British subject, and by profession a washerwoman, had incautiously wandered from Sierra Leone into the Siaccan dominions. It was alleged by Prince Manna that Mrs. Nelson's employer in Sierra Leone, a certain Mrs. Gray, owed him the sum of a hundred and fifty Spanish dollars, of which he was unable to obtain payment. It occurred to him that the forcible seizure and detention at Dombocorro of Mrs. Nelson might help him, and the lady and her child were accordingly detained. It is due to Mr. Manna— as his victim, refusing him his title, calls him in the letters she wrote to her husband and her employer in the British colony—to say that he did not otherwise harm her ; and his view that she was a chattel belonging to his debtor upon which he might levy a distraint would no doubt receive much local support at Gallinas. The woman's letters, however, came to the notice of the Governor of Sierra Leone, Sir Richard Doherty, with the result that he instructed the commander of H.M.S. *Wanderer*, Captain Denman, to take immediate steps, by force if necessary, for the release of Manna's captives. The Governor also delivered to Captain Denman a letter addressed to the bedridden old King to the effect that the Queen of England could by no means countenance the kidnapping of her subjects by members of His Majesty's family. This letter gave the gallant captain his opportunity. It was impossible, in his view, to ensure the receipt by Siacca of the official protest by forwarding it from the ship. The white slave-traders on the beach strongly objected to communications between their enemies, the ships of war outside, and their dear friends the native royalties inland. They had, indeed, announced their intention of using force to prevent any such communications, and, geographically at any rate, they were astride the line.

Denman had three ships under his command— the *Wanderer*, the *Rolla*, and the *Saracen*—and under pretext of delivering the letter and recovering Mrs. Nelson he determined upon a landing. On November 19th, 1840, a party of about a hundred seamen and marines, with three guns and a Congreve rocket apparatus, occupied Dombocorro without any opposition. The Spanish slave-merchants shrewdly cleared all but inanimate property out of the factories, though the sudden invasion of the English was not ostensibly concerned with their nefarious activities. The aged King, pleading his infirmities, sent word that the ingenious Manna and a family of mixed blood, named Rogers, would represent him; and a conference took place. Mr. Manna was promptly asked to produce Mrs. Nelson. He made a reply of some length, chiefly directed to aspersing the character of Mrs. Gray of Sierra Leone who owed him the dollars, but concluding with the assertion that he had two days before sent Mrs. Nelson back to her home. Unfortunately for this excuse, another scion of the royal house of Dombocorro, who was evidently a weaker brother, shortly afterwards appeared with the woman and her child and delivered them up to Denman. The imperturbable Manna thereupon apologised, but he evidently regarded the affair to the end as rather a pretty joke.

The object with which the landing had been made was now achieved; Captain Denman had recaptured his British subject in accordance with his instructions. But he found himself in force within the very nest of the slavers upon whom for some time past he had been keeping a tedious watch from outside. The opportunity was surely too good to be lost. Already the guns defending the factories had been promptly spiked by his bluejackets; and two days after the landing Captain Denman concluded a solemn treaty with Siacca (to which Manna and two members

of the Rogers family duly made their marks), by
which the King consented to the total destruction
of the barracoons and to the delivery to the
English of all slaves in the hands of the Spaniards.
In the circumstances the consent of the old chief
and his illiterate deputies should perhaps be
recorded with the aid of inverted commas : but
in return for his complaisance it was provided
that the cotton and the spirits in the factories
should be handed over to him " as being forfeited
in consequence of the owners having acted in
defiance of his law." The humour of crediting
King Siacca with abolitionist sympathies, and
even anti-slavery edicts, becomes more apparent
when we find that one of the factories was " listed "
as belonging to the Rogers branch of the royal
family. It is unlikely that Mr. Manna and his
relatives ever had again so unique an experience
of running with the hare and hunting with the
hounds. And burned the eight factories were,
on November 23rd and following days, with the
King's deputies looking on. In this proceeding
Prince Manna's ingenuity was again manifested ;
for although by the treaty Siacca, through his
deputies, undertook to destroy the barracoons
himself, Manna adroitly requested Captain Denman with his own hands to fire the two rockets
which began the demolition at Kamasura, and
that officer complied with the request. It was
clearly a useful thing to be able to report in case
the Spaniards made unpleasant remarks after the
English had gone. Afterwards nearly nine hundred slaves were handed over for transport to
Sierra Leone ; and quite an impressive little

scene must have been afforded by the boats of
the squadron taking chains, manacles, and other
incombustible instruments of slavery out beyond
the bar and dropping them into the sea.

Captain Denman gave a detailed account of
his proceedings to Sir Richard Doherty, who
sent it to Lord John Russell at the Colonial
Office. A report was also made to Captain
Tucker, the senior naval officer on the station,
who forwarded it to the Admiralty. Both the
Lords of the Admiralty and the Colonial Office
approved. Everything appeared to be in order.
The Foreign Office, writing to the Admiralty
in April, 1841, said it appeared to Lord Palmer-
ston that "no better plan could be pursued for
the suppression of the slave trade than a system
of blockade, combined with the destruction of
the factories on shore upon the plan pursued by
Captain Denman on the destruction of the slave
factories at the Gallinas." This pronouncement,
in spite of its wording, may be supposed to have
afforded a crumb of comfort to Captain Denman
when, in 1842, being then at home, he was served
with three writs claiming damages for trespass
to the tune of £130,000, £150,000, and £40,000
respectively, at the suit of the three Spanish
traders whose names have been given already.

When at last the law came to be looked into,
the previous decisions were not over-helpful.
In 1810 a vessel under Swedish colours and carrying
slaves had been captured by H.M.S. *Crocodile*
off the African coast, and her condemnation in
the Vice-Admiralty Court at Sierra Leone was
reversed on the ground that Sweden had not

abolished the slave trade. Ten years later the verdict of an English jury awarding £18,000 damages to a Spanish plaintiff in respect of lost profits on slaves in a brig taken by a British cruiser off Cape S. Paul had been upheld on appeal. It was by no means clear that Spain had forbidden the slave trade to her subjects in 1840. The Foreign Office consulted Her Majesty's Advocate-General in the Admiralty Court, and that gentleman's opinion emphasised an awkward situation. He said he could not take upon himself to advise that all the proceedings at Gallinas (and other places) were strictly justifiable. He thought the instructions which had been given to certain naval officers were such as could not with perfect legality be carried out; that the blockade of rivers, the destruction of buildings, and the carrying off of persons held in slavery in countries with which Great Britain was not at war could not be considered as sanctioned by the law of nations or the provisions of any existing treaties; and that however desirable it might be to put an end to the slave trade, " a good, however eminent, should not be obtained otherwise than by lawful means."

The case of Buron against Denman was a long time in coming to trial. There seems to have been an extraordinary difficulty in ascertaining what was the Spanish law with reference to slave-trading: at any rate there was trouble with a certain Don José Maria de Monreal, who could not be induced to give evidence about it before a commission duly appointed by the Court of Exchequer and sent out to Madrid, because he considered the commissioner his inferior in social rank, and resented the intrusion of an English Court. At length, in February, 1848, more than seven years after the events out of which it arose had taken place, the action was heard before four Barons of the Exchequer in a court " crowded to suffocation." The appearance of the Attorney-General as counsel for Captain Denman was an indication that the Government intended to make his cause their own. Counsel for the Spanish plaintiff began by inviting the jury to clear their minds of prejudice. He declared that supposing the defendant, having a conscientious objection to polygamy, had invaded some Eastern gentleman's seraglio and carried off the houris it contained, his action, though possibly more gratifying to himself, would have been neither more nor less illegal than was his interference with the Spaniards at Gallinas. The whimsical analogy was intended to put the jury in a good humour ; its correctness, however, could not be gainsaid. But fortunately the treaty which Denman had made with His Majesty King Siacca in the circumstances already described could be relied on to save the situation. It is, indeed, not quite clear whether some at least of the illegal acts did not precede the treaty ; but, waiving that point, the treaty had been ratified by Her Majesty's Government, and consequently such acts as were done under it became Acts of State for which the Government, and not the defendant, was responsible. In other words, the subsequent ratification of illegal acts was equivalent to a prior command to do them. Reasoning thus, the Court directed the jury to find for the defendant. It was ingenious, if not wholly convincing. Baron Parke was indeed constrained to point out that according to the common law the adoption of an agent's illegal act by a principal is quite different, since it does not free the agent from his own responsibility. But something had to be done ; and probably, though the maxim has been much criticised in England, the end justified the means.

X

THE ILLEANON PIRATES

A CERTAIN type of legislator never foresees that the statute which embodies his over-zeal in a possibly good cause is extremely likely to be used by the cynical for their own purposes. Excellent motives, doubtless, actuated the pro-moters of the drastic Act of Parliament passed in 1825, which made slave-trading by Englishmen piracy, and so a capital offence punishable by death. Yet the first prosecution under that enactment was instigated by some mutinous seamen against the captain of a merchant vessel in revenge for the disciplinary measures he had taken to keep them in order in the course of a voyage to the West Coast of Africa. Fortunately, however, the jury did not believe their allegation that the master had sold into slavery four ladies of colour who had come aboard as visitors. There was passed in the same year another Act of Parliament, equally well intentioned, aimed at the repression of foreign pirates : and the lavish bounties it offered, combined with its lack of sufficient safeguards against claims founded upon statements in the nature of things *ex parte*, laid it also open to abuse. At least, it may be said that in the claim made under this statute in respect of an affair between the boats of H.M.S.

Samarang and some piratical prahus off Gilolo
in the Moluccas in the year 1844, Captain Sir
Edward Belcher, C.B., as became a future Arctic
explorer, took every advantage of the openings
in the legislative ice ; and his story of the encounter with the Malays, upon which that claim was
based, is, let us say, well constructed to that end.
His victory in the Law Courts was as easy, and
at the same time as remarkable, as his mastery of
the pirates.   The sequel was the repeal of the
Act of Parliament, and the substitution for it of
one a good deal less accommodating.

It will be well first to state shortly the rich
promise of the Act of 1825 " for encouraging the
capture and destruction of Piratical ships or
Vessels."   It awarded to the officers and seamen
who should be on board any of His Majesty's
ships at such a capture or destruction the sum
of twenty pounds for each pirate taken or killed
during the attack, and five pounds for every
piratical person not taken or killed who should
have been on board the pirate vessel at the
beginning of the affair.   The counting of piratical
heads was not left entirely to a combatant
imagination ; there was added a formal provision,
which gave a semblance of strictness, that the
number of pirates should be proved by the
ship's papers found in the pirate vessel, or such
other evidence as the Judge of the Admiralty
Court might in the circumstances deem sufficient.
The idea that a pirate would have papers seems
a little naïve ; possibly the words had reference
to the fact that round about the year 1825 there
was in the West Indies a good deal of piracy,

more or less veiled by the use of letters of marque purporting to be issued by Spain's insurgent colonies. But the only reported claims for the head-money offered by this statute arise out of the destruction of the craft of marauding Malays twenty years later. Proof of numbers by ship's papers was not in such cases to be looked for ; and, as will appear, the Courts were oddly un-critical of the "other evidence" presented to them.

Sir Edward Belcher's little bill for 350 pirates killed at twenty pounds apiece and 980 others who escaped at five was supported by the affidavits of himself and three of his officers. When the petition was heard before Dr. Lushington, the Judge of the Admiralty Court, no opposition was offered, and he pronounced for the bounties allowed by the statute upon the estimate made by these gentlemen of the number of their antagonists. Thereupon there was a correspon-dence with the Treasury, which need not detain us, and a rather belated appeal to the Judicial Committee of the Privy Council, which was heard in June, 1849. Even then the number of pirates deposed to was not disputed ; the Admiralty contented themselves with arguing by their coun-sel that the piratical character of the vessels attacked and destroyed had not been established. All doubt on this point must be taken to have been set at rest by the judgment of the Judicial Committee, for that tribunal complimented the *Samarangs* upon their gallantry and allowed the claim. But it is seldom that a single ship's company has been able in peace time to earn a

H

bounty of nearly £12,000 within the space of
some four-and-twenty hours ; and it may be
of interest to follow the doings of the *Samarang's*
boats as they are set out in the petition presented
to the Court.

On the morning of June 3rd, 1844, according
to this document, the Captain left the *Samarang*,
then engaged in surveying duties near Gilolo,
for the purpose of fixing upon the chart the
position of a neighbouring island. He took with
him two boats, the gig, containing himself, the
master's assistant, and four seamen, and the
second barge, carrying twenty officers and men,
and landed upon a reef. Shortly after midday
what is described as an extraordinary yell indicated that the inhabitants of the island had
discovered the presence of the surveying party,
and a band of about forty savages, some naked
and some dressed in scarlet (of which more here-
after), was seen advancing from the land along
a reef, brandishing and hurling spears and arrows,
without, however, doing any damage to either
boats or crews. They were, says the report,
soon repulsed and put to flight by musketry.
Presently a prahu manned by fifteen natives
appeared coming round a point of the island to
look at the strangers from seaward, but not
liking the look of the brass six-pounder in the
bows of the barge it " sheered off much dis-
concerted " and rejoined the land forces of the
enemy at the back of the island without doing
anything—although their intention is stated nevertheless to have been " hostile." At three o'clock,
the naval party having finished their work with-

out further interference, Sir Edward decided to "retaliate this piece of treachery" as he phrases it. Accordingly the boats were rowed round, following the course the prahu had taken. They soon came in sight of it, as well as of another one filled with natives escaping from the village whence the first assailants had issued; and many other natives were observed running away into the jungle. Mr. Hooper, the purser, and the gig's crew were thereupon sent to burn the village and some boats lying upon the beach, a service they soon accomplished; whilst Sir Edward in the barge pursued the two prahus, and by means of doses of round and canister shot compelled their crews to run them ashore. The prahus, quite small affairs compared with those subsequently met with, were afterwards towed out to sea and burnt, and then the two ship's boats proceeded to a secluded bay some twenty miles away and anchored for the night.

They may be left there for the moment whilst we digress from the account placed before the Court to some supplementary details which Sir Edward, having no doubt the pending appeal in his mind, supplied in his *Narrative of the voyage of H.M.S. "Samarang,"* published in 1848. Desiring that there should be no question about the piratical character of his assailants he had made inquiries, and had been informed, he says, that "pirates only dress in scarlet or gay dresses, and that the peaceable traders of these seas invariably are clothed in dull plain colours." It sounds hardly wise of the pirates and a little hard on the peaceable trader, but to criticise the sumptuary regula-

tions of the Moluccas is not our business; and
Belcher's informant is corroborated by a compara-
tively recent book in which a story of an attack
by the pirates of those parts upon a trading brig,
apparently as late as the 'fifties or 'sixties of the
last century, describes their leader as conspicuous
in a scarlet dress. Belcher adds that the prahu
which had come round the corner to reconnoitre
hoisted a dirty Dutch flag, and after hailing
him in intelligible English and expressing a wish
to be allowed to proceed to a river somewhere
to the northward, went after all in quite another
direction. Whether he regarded the mere possession of an old Dutch ensign as a suspicious
circumstance he does not say; the conversation
had certainly nothing of the bold pirate about
it, and may well have been a ruse to gain time to
get out of range of the disconcerting six-pounder.
These details are only worth mentioning because
their very minuteness suggests some little un-
certainty in Sir Edward's mind. And except the
point made about piratical local colour, there is
so far little in the story that is inconsistent with
these natives being merely misguided objectors
to the invasion of their island for scientific purposes. But the English Courts about this time—
though perhaps Sir Edward did not know it—
seem to have been easily induced to believe in
pirates. In 1845 the case of *The Serhassan Pirates*
had come before them. This was a less inflated
claim under the same Act of Parliament in respect
of an attack in 1843 upon the boats of H.M.S.
Dido, notwithstanding that the boats displayed
what the reporter calls " a flag of truce, viz. a

blue ensign." In that case the Court not only scouted the suggestion that Malays might possibly not be quite clear about the British flag—we had only three ensigns in use in the Navy at this period—but, unless the reporter has erred in his description of the flag actually displayed, apparently thought that the failure of these savages to read into the blue ensign a meaning it never had either before or since was evidence, *inter alia*, of their piratical leanings. So that perhaps Sir Edward was wise in adducing all the smallest things he could think of.

We must now go back to the *Samarang's* barge and gig, left anchored close inshore in the secluded bay, and to the story of what happened to them as narrated in the petition to the Court. After what had occurred the day before, one is not surprised to learn that at 2 a.m. on the morning of the 4th the repose of the two boats' crews was cut very short by the sound of war-gongs. Five large prahus were seen bearing down upon them in the moonlight, the leading one highly decorated, and bearing " such streamers and banners as are borne only by the Illeanon pirates, the most noted pirates in these seas." What these banners were is not more precisely stated. The boats at once cleared for action. Then there was a short parley. A scarlet-clad figure hailed them from the roof or upper deck of the leading prahu, and asked who they were. " The Captain of a British ship of war," answered Sir Edward in Malay and English, whereupon the questioner in the prahu wanted to know where the ship was. " Outside," was the answer, perhaps as definite

a one as could be given, since the boats had
apparently not been back to their ship since
early on the previous day ; but thereupon the
chief and people in the prahus " commenced
yelling and capering " and casting spears and
shooting arrows into the boats. A dozen rounds
from the barge's gun, however, divided between
the prahus at a range of less than twenty yards,
soon caused the splinters to fly and completely
cleared the roofs. The three largest prahus were
first taken by the barge, towed out into deep water
—it appears that their crews in a panic had run
them ashore—and left in charge of Mr. Hooper
in the gig ; and then the Captain went in pursuit
of the other two, which after a chase of two miles
and a sharp conflict were also captured, the
survivors of their crews escaping to the shore.
But the affair was by no means finished. The
first quintet of prahus was but just disposed of,
it being now six o'clock in the morning, and the
two boats were still separated by the two miles
distance that the barge had gone in pursuit,
when another five prahus even larger than the
first lot put in an appearance. Quintet number
two promptly endeavoured to get between the
barge and the gig ; we might have supposed this
to imply a recognition on the pirates' part of the
weakness of scattered squadrons, but for the fact
that they failed so curiously to apply that elementary knowledge to the marshalling of their own
forces. The five new-comers were tackled by
the redoubtable barge at close range, and " by
discharges of round and canister shot from the
six-pounder gun, divided alternately amongst

them, together with Congreve rockets and musketry, great slaughter and confusion were caused,
and those of the pirates who were not killed or
severely wounded jumped overboard and fled
to the jungle for safety." It was during this
fight that a ball from one of the prahus struck
the rocket-stand in the barge and glancing off
wounded Sir Edward and knocked him overboard.
He was not seriously hurt, however, and upon
being pulled out of the water was able to resume
his command shortly afterwards. This was fortu-
nate, for yet another five prahus arrived on the
scene at this juncture. But the barge was short
of ammunition and had her commander wounded;
and no attempt to deal with this third five was
made for the present. Leaving the gig to look
after herself the barge steered for the *Samarang*,
then cruising, it was said, about a dozen miles
away.

We are next told that Mr. Hooper, thus left
alone in command of the gig, had leisure, notwithstanding the presence in his neighbourhood
of the new pirate flotilla, to examine the three
captured prahus from the first batch which, it
will be remembered, he had in his charge. He
found they were armed with guns, that they had
on board the important flags and banners which
showed them to be Illeanon pirates, and he found
in one of them a woman and a child, whom he
kindly put ashore. He also found just one dead
pirate; and having destroyed the craft he too
returned to the ship.

Meanwhile the barge, under Lieutenant Heard,
and now accompanied by the *Samarang's* two

cutters mounting a three-pounder apiece, came back to the scene of the morning's action. They found the five prahus from which the crews had been driven at that time—the second batch of five—hauled up in a creek and lying there with seven others equally large. Presumably these seven included the third five which had arrived just before the barge left for the ship: at any rate the whole of the twelve now found in the creek were attacked and destroyed. After visiting another creek and demolishing two small prahus found there with no one on board, and which therefore could not be included in the bill, the barge and cutters once more sought the *Samarang*.

The first thing that will probably strike the reader of this narrative is the obliging way in which the pirates turn up in successive batches small enough to be defeated by two boats and twenty-six officers and men. Even so the odds were considerable. The first lot which attacked at two in the morning carried between them, according to Belcher's estimate, 350 men. The second lot were larger and their combined crews were put at 450. The third batch of twelve prahus destroyed in the afternoon were said to have been manned by 500 pirates: in this later affair the number of the *Samarang's* people is uncertain, as we are not told how many the two cutters carried. But one cannot help remarking that these pirates were surprisingly inefficient warriors: only one seaman, in addition to the Captain, is anywhere stated to have been hurt in an encounter with an enemy thirteen hundred strong and provided with guns.

The return of the barge to the ship, leaving the small gig to look after herself, at the moment when " five fresh prahus " were seen advancing, may have been rendered unavoidable through the failure of her ammunition ; but it is strange that these prahus made no attempt to cut off the gig as the preceding lot had endeavoured to do. The point has no bearing upon the estimate of the numbers engaged, but in the absence of any explanation of their inaction it almost seems as if the petition had hurried these five into the theatre of war just, so to speak, for the sake of keeping the stage filled, and had then forgotten to give them a part to play. It is possible moreover approximately to estimate the length of time the gig must have been left unsupported. Entries in the log of the *Samarang* show that the barge on this return journey was sighted from the ship at 6.40 and that she came alongside at 9. Therefore, supposing that she had been only ten minutes on her way when sighted, she took two hours and a half to go from the battlefield to the ship. This squares pretty well with the statement in the petition that the *Samarang* was ten or twelve miles away. The barge got away again with the two cutters—we have still the authority of the log for this—at 10.15. She may not have taken as much as two and a half hours to return, as possibly the *Samarang* had been standing in towards the land meanwhile ; but the forenoon must have been nearly spent before the barge and cutters arrived at the scene of the early morning's operations. By the time they got to work it was undoubtedly afternoon.

So that these five undamaged and undefeated prahus, each having by Belcher's estimate forty pirates on board, had five clear hours in which to deal with a gig containing six men. At seven o'clock Mr. Hooper is quietly examining the three captured prahus from the first batch left in his custody. There are other matters, difficult to understand now in what we are told of this affair, which may have been capable of explanation at the time, though there does not seem to have been any cross-examination of anybody. If the second five prahus, whose combined crews were put at 450 in number, arrived at six o'clock as stated, their defeat was a smart piece of work; for the *Samarang* sighted the barge on her way back forty minutes later. The earlier five which were not so large and carried a hundred men less had occupied the attention of the boats for four hours. It is true that these were not only defeated but destroyed as well, whilst the destruction of the second lot was left over until the afternoon, when the three boats tackled the dozen prahus of that last engagement.

Although Sir Edward Belcher may have been more sure than we are of the number of his adversaries, he was, as we have already pointed out, a little dubious upon the piracy point, even after the fight; and that was of even greater moment than his arithmetic, since no money accrued upon the destruction of any number of persons who were not pirates. He tells us in his book how, falling in soon after the affair with a Dutch merchant schooner, the master of which came on board his ship, he questioned him very closely about the pirates which might be expected to frequent the neighbourhood. He even made a sketch for the Dutch skipper of one of the prahus lately encountered, and that worthy at once obligingly said that no vessel so large or armed for war belonged to " any of the petty authorities of the neighbouring states " or could be other than one of the dreaded Illeanons. Evidence thus obtained is more interesting than cogent ; and it is of interest to find that legitimate, if negligible, authority, as well as pirates, might be encountered afloat in those regions. But Belcher's hearsay about wolves' clothing was no doubt correct ; it only seems a pity that since his antagonists treated him with so much considera-tion for his numerical inferiority they did not also save him the doubt about their piratical character by hoisting the Jolly Roger, of which perhaps the Court might have taken judicial cognisance.

INDEX

MADE AND PRINTED IN GREAT BRITAIN
AT THE BOWERING PRESS, PLYMOUTH